MIDWAY
BRAVERY

Dennis Gaub

MIDWAY
BRAVERY

THE STORY OF THE U.S. ARMY PILOT WHOSE
FAMED FLIGHT HELPED WIN A DECISIVE
WORLD WAR II BATTLE

Treasure State Heritage Press
Billings, Montana

Published in the United States by Treasure State Heritage Press, Billings, Montana

Includes bibliographic references and index

ISBN 978-1-7338736-0-4

Cover design by Rob Perry

Table of Contents

Dedication

I dedicate this book to two members of the Greatest Generation. First, to my late father, William "Bill" Gaub, an Army infantryman who served in the Occupation Forces in Germany at the end of World War II. He came home to Montana, married, and with my mother raised me and five younger brothers and sisters to adulthood with enduring, solid values. And to someone I never knew, my father's cousin, Herbert Hoffer, a Marine who perished in the Pacific theater of World War II. They are my American heroes.

Preface

It's easy to say when and where the idea for this book burst forth. From those nuggets flow the "why" of the book.

On February 11, 2013, during my previous life as a proposal manager for one of the world's biggest software companies, I began a day of work from my home office in a town near Bozeman, Montana. As usual, I started my morning by streaming "Morning Edition," the National Public Radio news program carried by Yellowstone Public Radio, which broadcasts from Billings, Montana. My ears perked when I heard program host Robert Siegel start a news segment:

"People used to ask Jim Muri about the 4th of June 1942. And, according to his family, he tended to be surprised by their interest. On that day, Mr. Muri, who died earlier this month at age 94, was a B-26 bomber pilot in World War II."

Siegel continued by telling how Muri and his six-man crew carried out an audacious attack against a Japanese carrier group sailing toward Midway Atoll. The carriers were part of a massive fleet which the Japanese Navy planned to use to invade and take over the atoll. The Japanese could have used Midway as a springboard for further strikes against the U.S., still reeling from the December 7, 1941, surprise attack on Pearl Harbor.

"Their ensuing torpedo run became the stuff of legend. Jim Muri's plane was riddled with anti-aircraft fire as he flew toward a Japanese carrier, then he had to fly back (to Midway), pursued by Japanese planes firing at him," Siegel said. The NPR newsman said a YouTube video described how Muri avoided being shot down and killed, along with his crew, in the Pacific Ocean. Muri's spur-of-the-moment lifesaving decision was to fly his bomber the length

9

of the carrier, so low that had he put down the plane's wheels, they could have touched the deck. Thus, the plane avoided enemy fire long enough to escape and return to the American base.

Siegel followed with an interview with Muri's daughter, Sylvia Saadati, in which she recalled stories she heard about her father's heroism.

I rushed out of my office and found my wife, a retired school librarian, seated in the front room of our house, gazing at a winter scene outside.

I summarized what I had heard, then said, "I wonder if this Muri guy is related to the Muris I knew in high school in Miles City (Montana)."

That prompted three fateful words from my wife, who met me after my career as a daily newspaper reporter ended but who knew I yearned to write in a creative mode again.

"There's your book."

More than anyone else, my late wife, the woman I loved for the past two decades, inspired this book. Steadfast, supportive and always willing to hear the latest wrinkles in my stories, she is the partner any writer wants and deserves.

Carolyn's prod started me on a long path to this book. The first stop was 300 miles away in Miles City. I phoned Kathy (Muri) Boutelle; she, her husband, Laurie, and I were classmates at Custer County High School from our freshman year through early in my junior year. My family then moved to Billings, where I graduated from Billings West High School.

I confirmed the connection I wondered about: Kathy was a niece of James P. (Jim) Muri, part of a large family with many members in Montana plus others scattered across the U.S. Kathy connected me with her cousin Sylvia, who put me in touch with her brother, James R. Muri, Jim and Alice Muri's older child, who lives in the Seattle-Tacoma area.

Next, over the 2013 Memorial Day weekend, Kathy invited my wife and me to a Muri family get-together, in Miles City at the home of Bill Muri, the oldest of a family of nine children (seven boys and two girls) and the brother ahead of Jim Muri in order of birth. Bill, a widower, died at age 98 in 2014. Others there that day included the Muri brothers' only living sister, Marie "Toots" Ansoms; and the three youngest brothers, Al ("Buck"), Pete and Karl. Pete and Karl have since died, but as of this writing (early March 2019), Buck is still alive and lives near Kathy, his daughter. Marie, a widow, lives in California.

Kathy, thank you for everything!

Among those who deserve credit for bringing this story to life, I think first of Sylvia and James. They displayed unlimited patience and gave of their time to relate stories about their parents. Besides Jim's military stories, they shared memories of that remarkable place, Montana's Great Plains, that fostered the man they called Dad and who became a hero to the American public during the dark, early months of World War II.

Thanks are due also to Jim and Alice Muri's grandson, Josh Muri, and his wife, Claudia, for their hospitality when my wife and I visited their home in Clackamas, Washington. After dinner, Josh guided me through artifacts of his grandfather's military career, now entrusted to him.

I salute a retired Navy officer and Annapolis graduate for the understanding he shared of the tricky but stellar bomber that Jim Muri piloted, the B-26 Martin Marauder. Marshall Magruder owns direct knowledge of the plane because his father, Peyton Magruder, was lead designer of the B-26 for the Glenn Martin Co. in the late 1930s. Marshall enjoys pointing out he was a passenger on the maiden Marauder flight in 1940, as an infant in his mother's arms.

Through Marshall and Sylvia, I learned about the B-26 Marauder Historical Society, an organization devoted to preserving the legacy of what some say might have been the best American plane in World War II. The society's mandate includes honoring those who piloted B-26s, served as crew members on the airships, handled ground maintenance and built Marauders at Martin plants in Baltimore and Omaha. My wife and I enjoyed attending the society's annual gathering in 2018 in Colorado Springs and hope to attend future gatherings.

We have said farewell to almost all the "first generation" society members, those involved in getting B-26s to combat missions in the Pacific and European theaters in World War II. Yet, their children, grandchildren, great-grandchildren and others who appreciate what the Marauder men — and women — meant to the war effort and American freedom are preserving a proud legacy.

Three descendants of two of the most famous figures in military aviation during World War II provided assistance. Two of Jimmy Doolittle's grandchildren, Jimmy Doolittle III and his cousin, Jonna Doolittle Hoppes, and Robert Arnold, grandson of Army Air Force Chief of Staff Henry "Hap" Arnold, replied to emails from a stranger in Montana. They took time to critique a section of the book dealing with their forebears. Thank you.

Thanks, Craig Swartz, for sharing the wartime diary, photos and other material pertaining to your uncle, Henry "Hank" Swartz, Jim

Muri's best friend in high school and a man you never knew. Your appreciation of your Eastern Montana heritage is laudable.

Chapter 20 represents sheer authorial fun, one of the most enjoyable writing experiences I've had since becoming a journalist 50 years ago. The songwriting and storytelling talents of World War II Navy veteran Lonnie Bell, who celebrates his 95th birthday in July 2019, made it possible. Stay forever young, friend!

Early in the journey this book represents and along the winding road it followed, I contacted Jean Nielsen, archivist at the Miles City Public Library. She answered inquiries and emailed material that provided insight into Jim Muri's early years.

My narrative gained added richness from diaries found in two books about 22nd Bomb Group airmen, whose ranks included Jim Muri and his best friend in the Army Air Force, Merrill "Jo Jo" Dewan. Thank you, Tom Dewan, for giving me permission to quote diary entries at length from your 2009 book about your father, "Red Raider Diary." Also, thanks to Mike Edmonds, vice-president of the 22nd Bomb, for permitting me to quote portions of diaries written by 22nd members found in a 2006 book, "Revenge of the Red Raiders," volume 1 of the association's illustrated history of the 22nd's missions during World War II.

Access to wartime flight records for Jimmy Doolittle and Jim Muri enhanced my project. I thank researcher Bill Biegel, who found Muri's logbook, and James Scott, author of the 2016 book, "Target Tokyo: Jimmy Doolittle and the Raid That Avenged Pearl Harbor," who provided Doolittle's logbook.

My two sons, Julian and Brian, encouraged my writing. To them, thanks and good luck as you pursue your passions.

Bravo to my developmental editor, Craig Lancaster, who gave

the same quality polish to this book as he did to my first one.

This narrative summarizes the documented life of Jim Muri. It contains dialogue found in sources such as newspaper and magazine articles, books, interviews, personal conversations and the like, which is within quote marks and is cited either in the text (newspaper articles) or in the notes. For the sake of narrative flow, additional dialogue has been added, also within quote marks but not cited in the notes. I've made this dialogue as true to the times, the situations and the personalities portrayed as possible.

Errors of fact and interpretation are mine.

Introduction - Mystery Mission

A bugle sounded as a Marine raised the American flag. The stars and stripes fluttered in the gentle breeze rolling in from the Pacific. Reveille roused Jim Muri at 3 a.m. on a day in early June 1942 that shaped his life.

He sat up, stretched, rubbed the sleep out of his eyes, and brushed sand off his Army Air Force uniform. Then the lanky young pilot stood up to his full 6-foot-4 stature, bending under the wing of his B-26 bomber, which had sheltered him while he slept a few hours. His eyes adjusted to the pitch dark.

Muri, accustomed to quiet nights at his parents' ranch on Montana's Great Plains, awoke to the clattering of albatrosses. It was prime mating season for "gooney birds," as servicemen called the white, ocean-going birds. Day and night, thousands of them grunted, moaned, screamed, whistled and scraped their bills in a mating dance. It took some getting used to hearing and seeing their courtship show. As it had for millennia, the ritual took place on scrub grass near the sandy beach of Eastern Island, a 336-acre dot of land in the central Pacific.

Other members of Muri's crew heard the wake-up call and now stood nearby, stretching and rubbing their eyes. They, too, had slept as best they could outdoors, sheltered by their plane on a balmy night. The group included co-pilot P.L "Pren" Moore and five other men ready for duty in the early months of World War II. Six days earlier, on May 29, they had flown the twin-engine medium bomber 1,100 miles from Hickam Field on Hawaii's Oahu island to an atoll at the far north end of the Hawaiian chain. Their ultimate destination, Midway, comprised four islands clustered around a coral reef; Eastern Island, the second-largest, was where the Navy had constructed three runways to serve Army, Marine and Navy planes in 1941. Barracks and a mess hall, also built then, completed the atoll's conversion into a naval air station.

Why are we here? Muri wondered. The other young fliers, ranging in age from 21-year-old tail gunner Earl Ashley to 23-year-old Muri and 24-year-old P.L. Moore to the "old men" of the group, William Moore and John Gogoj, 26 and 33, pondered the same question. They and all Americans knew the U.S. was at war with the Axis powers — Japan, Germany, and Italy. America's efforts to stay neutral ended on December 7, 1941, with Japan's devastating surprise attack on Pearl Harbor, which prompted the U.S. to declare war on Japan. Germany and Italy seized that declaration as justification to declare war on the U.S., which joined Great Britain and the Soviet Union as the Allied powers battling Germany and Italy, the Axis combatants in Europe and North Africa. The English and the U.S. now led the war effort in the Pacific against the third Axis power, Japan. The Dutch were gone, having surrendered their East Indies colonies to the ascendant Asian power.

Six months after Pearl Harbor, Muri and his crew were among thousands of American sailors, soldiers, and fliers stationed in the Pacific. All knew or sensed that combat against Japan's juggernaut was inevitable. How Midway fit into the strategic puzzle, though, was a mystery to Muri and his fellow servicemen. Promoted that spring to first lieutenant — he expressed surprise at the bump in rank in a letter to his wife, Alice— Muri felt like a pawn in an oceanic chess game. U.S. Admiral Chester Nimitz and Japanese

Admiral Isoroku Yamamoto, commanders of opposing naval forces in the Pacific, moved the pieces in this life-and-death contest.

Untested in battle — they had never fired a shot in combat — Muri and his crew shared a mixture of excitement and unease during six days of suspense on Midway. On June 4, 1942, they waited for daylight, their minds focused on the increasing likelihood that this day would bring their first wartime mission.

The scene was chaotic. Overnight, Navy PBY scout planes carried out a torpedo run and spotted Japanese shipping, but the vessels the American fliers saw were not what battle planners considered the prized target: Japan's aircraft carriers, best in the world.

At 4 a.m. on June 4th, Muri and his crew, and the pilots and crews of the three other B-26s parked along the airstrip, heard the rumble of Navy scout planes starting up. Eleven Catalina PBYs took to the air, searching for the approaching Japanese fleet.

Midway buzzed with activity. Telephones rang. Officers barked orders to those not already at assigned defensive posts: Man your stations!

It was still too dark to see, but the Marauder men could hear 16 big bombers warming up, B-17 Flying Fortresses launched to hit the Japanese from high altitude. (This mission failed.)

Then came electrifying news, a 5:45 a.m. radio message from a Catalina scout plane that had spotted two Japanese carriers sailing about 200 miles northwest of Midway. The main body of the fleet was in range.

The pilot of another Navy scout plane saw dozens of Japanese fighters and bombers, launched from the carriers, speeding toward the American base. He had no time to encrypt his message, sent in the clear but only to Navy radios: "Many airplanes heading Midway, bearing 320, distance 150."

Captain Jim Collins, a Louisianan who commanded the B-26s, told his airmen to check their planes again. A few gulped coffee while they anticipated immediate action.

Collins told what happened next.

"At 6:15, a messenger in a speeding Jeep brought me a note giving the position of our target and its distance." Jo Warner, an Army officer serving as a liaison between Nimitz's command and the Army fliers on temporary duty at the atoll, delivered the message.

"Japanese planes are inbound. We've spotted the enemy fleet," Warner said.

As light broke over the Pacific, the top brass at Midway and on two U.S. carriers off Midway harbored no doubt that beyond the horizon lay the Japanese carriers. This was the prize Americans had sought since breaking Japan's code and learning of the island nation's plans to invade Midway. Commanding officers, however, left low-ranking officers like Muri guessing about the foe they would confront. All they got was a vague hint of Japanese shipping they were to hit in the Pacific.

"Your target's at 320 degrees, 150 miles out," Warner shouted. "Go."

The din of dozens of warming-up warplanes grew louder. Six Navy Avenger torpedo planes took off first. Then four B-26 bombers thundered down the runway and into the sky. The B-26s at Midway carried torpedoes, and so did ten B-26s defending the Aleutians against a diversionary attack by the Japanese on the same day. It was the only time planes flown by the Army Air Force, or by its successor, the Air Force, ever used torpedoes in combat.

Jim Muri, as pilot of *Susie-Q*, the nickname of his bomber, joined a wave of 10 Army and Navy planes that took off from Midway from 6 a.m. to 6:15 a.m. Unbeknownst to the young pilots, they faced overwhelming odds.

As noted Midway author Walter Lord wrote, "How could this huge armada lose?" The Japanese fleet, totaling about 190 ships, included 11 battleships, eight carriers, 23 cruisers, 65 destroyers and dozens of support vessels. It sailed in an 1,800-mile arc across the Pacific. The Japanese Navy deployed 700 planes, 261 on the carriers headed for Midway, and it sent 100,000 men into battle commanded by twenty admirals who reported to Yamamoto atop the pyramid.

Yet, Muri joined 27 other Army airmen and 18 Navy fliers, a combined 46 scared young Americans, who carried out the initial U.S. attack against Japan's massive fleet. They wrote the first chapter of the story of one of the greatest naval battles in world history.

Muri, a dark-haired Montanan with an Errol Flynn-inspired mustache he and the other B-26 pilots had grown to distinguish themselves from the Navy pilots, graduated from high school in 1936 and enlisted in the Army. In those early-morning hours on June 4, 1942, he hoped six years in the military had prepared him for whatever lay ahead. As the second-oldest son of a first-generation Norwegian immigrant and his second-generation German-Swedish immigrant wife, he was half a world away from his roots. He and his six brothers and two sisters helped their parents work a combined cattle ranch-farm in drought-stricken,

19

Depression-era Eastern Montana. There, catching and breaking broncs running wild represented high-adrenaline danger. He never brushed with death in rural Montana, but things would change on that spring morning in 1942. That was when Muri piloted his bomber across the Pacific, running a gauntlet of dozens of Japanese fighter planes and ships blasting a barrage of bullets, cannon shells and anti-aircraft flak.

Jim Muri's bravery on the morning of June 4, 1942, would earn him the Distinguished Service Cross, second only to the Medal of Honor in prestige among Army combat awards. His life began in the high plains region between the Yellowstone and Missouri rivers.

Chapter 1 - The Man from Montana

"Hey, Jim, it's too hot. Let's cool off. Race you to the river!"

The cry rang out on a scorching summer afternoon when Jim Muri and the three brothers closest to him in age, Bill, Andy and Bob, decided they had to beat the heat. Those Muris, plus three younger brothers and two sisters — nine children total — grew up in Carterville, an Eastern Montana ranching community. Jim and his brothers attended and graduated from high school in the region's de facto city, Miles City, which had a population of 7,175 in the 1930 census. Both places lie along the Yellowstone River, a rough-and-tumble stream that meanders through and shapes the Great Plains landscape.

North of the Yellowstone, buttes, badlands and arroyos spread across millions of acres of open space. Cattle and horses grazed; antelope and mule deer foraged; and coyotes roamed a vast place that still had a feel of the frontier. All that sparsely populated land also furnished a place for the Muri youngsters to engage in youthful high jinks and build lasting memories of home.

This place became a magnet that drew Jim back to Montana. Almost 40 years after he left, Jim returned to the Yellowstone River valley. In his early 50s and retired from the Air Force, Muri and his wife moved from the West Coast to the Treasure State. They lived for 30 years on a small ranch in south-central Montana, in the shadow of the state's highest mountains and close to the iconic waterway.

The Yellowstone was a fixture of life for people in Carterville. Ice jams sometimes caused lowland flooding in late winter. During spring runoff, snowmelt in the Rockies made the river run deep and fast, its current pounding, the torrent carrying cottonwood trees yanked from the banks for miles before dropping them in the river bottom. As the summer wore on, the Yellowstone tamed to an almost placid flow, making it possible some years in the drought-ridden 1930s for people to walk across the river at downstream spots.

Carterville lay about two-thirds of the way along the Yellowstone's total 692-mile course, which starts in the Wyoming wilderness south of Yellowstone National Park and ends just inside North Dakota, where it joins the Missouri River. In Jim's youth and today, only irrigation diversion dams jutted into the Yellowstone, making it the longest undammed river in the lower 48 states.

The Yellowstone functioned as a transportation corridor for millennia. First came Indians paddling their canoes up and down the river, followed by Lewis and Clark, navigating downstream towards St. Louis at the end of their 1803-06 expedition. Soon, fur trappers and traders poled mackinaws and keelboats, loaded with beaver pelts that would become hats worn by the fashionable in Eastern U.S. and European cities. Before Carterville existed, its location where the Rosebud River fed into the Yellowstone became Fort Alexander, which served the American Fur Company for 11 years in the mid-19th century. Shallow-draft steamboats risked the Yellowstone in the 1870s and 1880s.

Carterville (or Cartersville — names for the town were often mixed and still are mixed in conversation) exemplified the boosterism and unbridled optimism that swept Eastern Montana at the start of the 20th century. Early arrivers named the town for

Thomas H. Carter, a U.S. senator from Montana who helped to reclaim a large plat of arid, sagebrush-covered land in the area to make it suitable for irrigated crops such as sugar beets. Carter also platted the Carterville town site.

By the time Jim Muri was born, two railroads, the Northern Pacific and Milwaukee Road, snaked across the Great Plains from Chicago and the Twin Cities toward Seattle. Parts of their routes hugged the Yellowstone. The Milwaukee built a depot in Carterville in 1907, so its passenger trains were a familiar sight to Jim and the community. Carterville got a post office two years later; it closed in 1957.

Automobile travel boomed in the U.S. after World War I, and by the mid-1920s, an all-weather, cross-country highway, the Yellowstone Trail, followed the Yellowstone Valley. That highway became U.S. Highway 10, which in crossing Montana ran through Rosebud, south of Carterville. Interstates 94 and 90, built in the 1960s and 1970s, replaced Highway 10.

Finally came airplanes. When commercial flights appeared over Carterville, they sparked the imagination of Jim Muri, whose roots in the area dated to the 1880s.

That was when his maternal grandfather, Carl W. Johnson, arrived in what became Rosebud County. Johnson had migrated from Sweden in 1877. He married Mary Bachhaus in 1894; she had come from Germany in 1892. Some family members say she was a nanny in the court of Kaiser Wilhelm II, Germany's king, before coming to America.

Carl and Mary Johnson claimed a homestead of 160 acres where they farmed.

The Johnson home became a frequent visiting spot for friends and neighbors traveling to and from Miles City, 40 miles away. The visitors included members of the Cheyenne tribe, which occupied a reservation in the southern part of Rosebud County. Mary Johnson told Jim and other grandchildren stories about Two Moons, a prominent member of the tribe who often visited her home.

The Johnsons had two daughters, Nellie, born in 1896, and Hannah, born in 1901; Carl Johnson died in 1915, so Jim never knew that grandfather. Mary Johnson, a widow for almost three decades, moved to Miles City, where she died in 1945.

Jim Muri's father, Rasmus "R.P." Muri, migrated from Norway to the United States in 1906. When he came to Montana, he first lived in Hathaway, another Rosebud County hamlet, and worked for the Northern Pacific Railroad. Later, he helped prepare semi-arid land on the north side of the Yellowstone River for irrigation. R.P. Muri married Nellie Johnson in 1915, and they farmed their own land.

The couple moved to Nellie's parents' farm in 1920 and lived there the rest of their lives. They raised nine children: seven boys and two girls born in 19 years, ranging from William, born in 1916, and Jim, born in 1918, to Pete, the youngest, born in 1935. Children in between were Robert, Andy, Marie ("Toots"), Alfred ("Buck"), Anna Mae and Karl. As the family grew, so did the R.P. and Nellie Muri spread, which eventually encompassed nine sections of land, about 5,700 acres.

Friends and family remembered R.P. Muri as the man who dropped his line from the old Rosebud Bridge into the Yellowstone River and hauled in a lot of fish before his death in 1969. Locals remembered Nellie Muri for tending the Carterville booth at the Rosebud County Fair in Forsyth for many years. She died in 1974.

Although flying later caught Jim Muri's imagination, it likely seemed a farfetched notion to him in the late 1920s and early 1930s. Commercial amusement was limited; TV didn't exist and just a handful of radio stations served Montana listeners. Carterville never amounted to much, even by Montana standards. Besides the train depot, the hamlet had a general store with a bar; that building also served as the post office. Residents danced at the local community hall. No churches took root.

The closest town, Rosebud, a few miles away, had a movie theater, but its existence was precarious during the Great Depression. Rosebud also boasted a bandstand where on summer nights a community band played. That entertainment ended by the time Jim was 10 or 11 because residents moved the bandstand near what became U.S. Highway 10 and used it as a kitchen that served meals to motorists.

If the Muri family got to the Rosebud County seat, Forsyth, during county fair time, they could take in the rodeo and horse racing on a half-mile straight track.

"Hey, Jim, did you hear? Jack Dempsey's coming to town," a friend said.

Muri could have heard the buzz when he was an eighth grader at the Carterville school. The talk in nearby Miles City was about the possibility that the Manassas Mauler was coming there.

In January 1932, the *Miles City* (MT) *Daily Star* reported that its sports editor received a telegram from Sioux City, Iowa. The sender, Tom Brisbane, was said to be handling arrangements for boxing matches by Dempsey, the former world heavyweight champion, who was on a "comeback campaign" in 1931 and 1932.

The telegram said: "Will book Dempsey in your city for February. Will box six rounds any opponent you may select or will box three opponents two [rounds] of each. If you are interested, advise. Also stating [sic] seating capacity of your coliseum."

The telegraph contained a catch: "Providing satisfactory arrangements can be made with your local promoter."

The *Star's* sports editor gave the telegram to Bob Senate, "local widely known sportsman," who answered the wire. Senate asked for details and what payment Dempsey expected for the exhibition match.

Star readers learned Dempsey was coming to Montana later in the year. He reportedly was scheduled to referee a boxing program at the fair in Great Falls. Research uncovered no further mention of this purported Dempsey visit to Montana.

Even idle talk of a Dempsey visit to Miles City probably would have stirred interest among Jim and his brothers. Boxing was one of the country's most popular sports, and its reach extended to Carterville. In March 1940, the next two brothers behind Jim, Andy and Bob, won district championships in the southeastern Montana Golden Gloves tournament in Billings. Bob won the 147-pound title, and Andy excelled in the light heavyweight (175-pound) class. Tournament officials voted him the hardest puncher in the tournament. Bob's feats that year included beating the 1939 state middleweight Golden Gloves champion, Walt Baylor of Winnett, according to the *Great Falls (MT) Tribune* (March 23, 1940).

Their showing in Billings sent Bob and Andy to the state tournament in Great Falls. Andy fared best. He won his semifinal match, a decision over Dick Dorsey of Chinook. He lost an "unpopular decision" to Leo Bens of Butte in the championship match. Andy went down for a nine-count in the second round "but came back to rock Bens with wicked lefts. The early lead by Bens proved the winning margin," according to the *Tribune* (March 31, 1940).

Adventure in the Montana outdoors also beckoned, and the Muris answered. When their parents went to Forsyth to get groceries or other supplies, the older brothers staged impromptu roundups.

"We'd run the cattle in the corral, so you'd have a rodeo. They'd buck like hell," Bill Muri said.

His brothers Bob and Andy would saddle the milk cows, climb on and "jump, jump, jump. They'd ride 'em, and we couldn't, Jim and I. ... They'd come out of there and off we'd go" into the surrounding hills.

One cowboy experience that stood out from the rest occurred on a spring day in the early 1930s. Jim, Bill and Bob galloped their horses along Big Jack Creek, which wound through the Muri ranch before draining into the Yellowstone.

Jim prodded his horse alongside Bill's.

"I can ride any cow there is," Jim boasted.

His brothers called Jim's bet, roped a cow and put his saddle on the bovine. Jim climbed on.

"He rode about three or four jumps [of the cow], and off he went," Bill Muri recalled.

"Here we had a cow running free with his saddle. Bob went up to catch the cow, and he caught the saddle horn with his rope," Bill said, but the adventure continued.

The spooked cow dashed over the hill and into one of the side draws that break up the erosion-pocked sandstone landscape of Montana's Great Plains. Bob, riding his trusty horse, Ole Pete, finally caught up with the cow. He roped her to a halt, but the runaway animal skinned her side during the chase.

"In about a week or two, we were having branding, and dad said, 'I wonder what happened to that cow?' " Bill said. Bob replied, "I betcha that's some kind of disease."

Growing up, Jim and his brothers had mongrel dogs as pets. The dogs couldn't resist tangling with rattlesnakes when they emerged from hibernation in early spring and coiled on rocks to soak up the warm sun.

Often the dogs killed snakes, but they risked being bit, according to an undated letter that a longtime Eastern Montana friend sent Jim years after both men's boyhood. The venom would cause the dogs' heads to swell, so they would retreat to the mud in irrigation ditches and wallow there for days. In time, the fever from snake bites abated, and the dogs recovered, ready to kill more snakes.

Jim and his siblings rode horses or walked to the elementary school in Carterville; school buses were uncommon. The one-room schoolhouse educated students ranging in age from six to 14 or 15, according to Bill Muri.

"The teacher either had control or they didn't last long. We learned the basics, plus penmanship," he said.

The Muris received consistent discipline at and away from school. "If we got a licking at school, we got another when we got home, so we learned early to do as we were told," he said.

Students got hot lunches in the winter when their parents took turns bringing hot cocoa or soup, which someone rewarmed on a big coal heating stove in the school room.

In the spring, if rain came, Jim and his brothers and sisters walked or rode horses through a landscape awash in the colors of blooming wildflowers: bluebells, wild roses, lupine, and flowering prickly pear cactus. The strong aroma of sagebrush filled their noses. They heard meadowlarks whistle and warble from fenceposts and listened to the cry of killdeers trying to draw predators away from their young. Sometimes they spotted gulls foraging through plowed fields for insects and worms.

The Muri children rarely missed school. Jim and Andy, for example, earned certificates for eight months perfect attendance toward the end of the 1931-32 school year, according to the *Billings* (MT) *Gazette* (May 14, 1932).

On warm nights, with windows open, the Muris could hear crickets chirping and the loud buzzing of cicadas. Sometimes, just before falling asleep, they heard the whistle of a locomotive in the night, a Milwaukee Railroad passenger train passing through Carterville.

When Jim and his brothers rode their horses north, they sensed the hugeness of the land. "You probably could have rode all the way to the Missouri River without opening a gate," Bill Muri said of that era. Many homesteads, with fences marking boundaries, existed, but "lots of open range" still existed. A schoolhouse stood every 10 miles in almost every direction, testimony to settlers' belief in the value of education.

Amid the Great Depression, Jim Muri and his brothers and sisters found an outlet for youthful energy. Good-natured give and take was the norm. "We never had real battles — well, we never whacked each other's eyes out or anything. You know how kids are," Bill Muri said.

Another memorable adventure occurred on a summer day in the 1930s, as the mercury topped 100 degrees and Jim and his brothers sought relief from heat that baked the plains. A cottonwood tree spread its foliage across an irrigation ditch that brought water from the Yellowstone River. The brothers began skinny dipping. They tied a rope to a tire, which they suspended from the tree branches so they could swing across the ditch.

"We'd catch each other, but the time I went across, Jim moved over and I hit the tree. Down the ditch we went," Bill said. Oops. A group of girls were watching, so "we went back up the river," he said.

The Muri brothers' escapades — especially those of Bob and Andy — remained vivid in the mind of their sister, Marie. The pair "always did things together," she said during a July 29, 2018, conversation in Laurel, Montana. "They were like the Katzenjammer kids," the two characters in a comic strip popularized by U.S. newspapers in the early 1900s.

As Jim grew up, he saw the last hurrah of Montana's frontier days play out in two iconic images: sheep grazing in the nearby hills, their fleece destined to make the Treasure State a top supplier of wool to the world; and thousands of horses thundering through the badlands.

Each fall, flocks of sheep passed Carterville as sheepherders drove them south toward the Yellowstone Valley to winter range. The drive repeated in the spring, when herders trailed the sheep north to summer range.

The sight of horses on the Montana range in the 1930s was spectacular. A famed outfit, Chappel Brothers Cannery, ran 60,000

30

horses over a third of Montana, including land north of the Muri home. Jim saw herds of horses bearing the CBC brand being moved from the open range through Carterville. Every spring, the young Muris would ride out and round up a few of their favorite horses for use during the warmer months to help with transportation and cultivation. Then, as fall approached, they released the horses again.

In the late 1930s, the last herd of CBC horses crossed the Rosebud Bridge over the Yellowstone. It was the end of an era.

Unlike the wild horses, Carterville didn't fade away. Whatever high hopes the early-day senator from Montana and other held for the town never materialized. Yet, it didn't become a ghost town, although years of drought and the post-World War I crash in commodity prices doomed Carterville to become a wide spot in the road, which it remains today.

Chapter 2 - Eyes on the Sky

Jim Muri was an infant when a young Miles City man, then finishing high school, caught the flying bug that would bite Muri. His role model, trailblazer pilot Frank Wiley, found his life's destiny on a never-to-be-forgotten day in high school, he said in a book he wrote decades later.

"I was sitting in a high school class at the Custer County High School in 1919, on a warm fall day, gazing out of the window with characteristic inattention, when I became aware of an unusual sound, which could be identified only as coming from a high-powered airplane engine."

Its engines rumbling as it flew over Miles City, a "huge" plane drew Wiley and his "uncontrollable" classmates to the window. They saw a twin-engine Army bomber fly west and land in an open field near Fort Keogh. The fort, an Army outpost built after the Battle of the Little Bighorn in 1876, later became an agricultural experiment station.

Col. R.S. Hartz commanded the Martin MB-1 bomber, which had a four-man crew. It came to Miles City during an "around the rim" flight, which took it 9,283 miles around the border of the U.S. Hartz and his men made 100 stops in 31 states, including four in Montana. The bomber, which had a top speed of 105 mph and could climb to 10,000 feet, was on a trip planned by the plane's designer, Glenn Martin, to prove air travel was safe and thus to boost commercial flight. Success on the 1919 flight helped make Americans aware that airplanes were a viable means of transportation.

By 1930, airlines followed the Yellowstone River, making scheduled stops in Glendive, Miles City, Billings, Butte and

Missoula, and later Helena, en route between Minneapolis and Seattle. Thus, all Jim Muri had to do to imagine flying an airplane was to crane his neck upward.

As a teenager, Muri could take a break from his ranch chores and gaze up at one of the Ford Tri-Motor airplanes that droned over his parents' ranch. Nicknamed the "Tin Goose," they were one of the early aircraft that appeared in the endless sky above Carterville. Northwest Airlines first used Tri-Motors, which carried eight or nine passengers plus mail, on flights from Chicago to Seattle. Three flights per day connected Miles City with Minneapolis and Chicago to the east and Seattle to the west. The planes weren't fast; powered by three Curtis-Wright radial engines, they cruised at about 105 mph, but they were reliable workhorses and straightforward to fly, with a range of almost 600 miles.

Though the Tin Goose had a ceiling of about 18,000 feet, planes that caught Muri's eye weren't flying that high as they traversed the breaks, buttes and badlands of Rosebud County. In those days before modern navigational aids, Northwest pilots watched for railroad tracks next to the Yellowstone River and followed them to stay on course as they wended their way across Montana's vast open spaces.

As he continued his upward gaze, Jim thought, that plane could be in Seattle by morning. He told himself, one day, I want to fly one of those machines.

From the fall of 1932 through May 1936, Jim attended high school in Miles City and lived during the week at the modest home of his grandmother, Mary Johnson, helping the widow with household tasks. Older brother Bill also lived with the boys' grandmother until he graduated from high school in the spring of

1934, and younger brothers Bob, Andy and Al "Buck" followed in their older siblings' footsteps. Jim and his brothers traveled 40 miles to the Miles City school because it had a Future Farmers of America (FFA) chapter, unavailable at nearby Rosebud High School.

Although Jim Muri dreamed about a future as an airplane pilot, he focused on day-to-day life on the Great Plains. His father gave Jim sage advice. The senior Muri, who couldn't speak a word of English when he first came to America, stressed how important it was to communicate. Rasmus "understood the complications of communications barriers and shared his experiences with his children so they could learn from his challenges and his mistakes."

Rasmus also taught Jim "how to be resourceful and take full advantage of his environment," a lesson that would guide Jim throughout his 94 years. Jim explored the rugged surroundings of his part of Montana, which still had a newly-settled spirit a half-century after it achieved statehood. Horses and horseback riding became an early avocation, and something that lasted a lifetime. One could see hard times and shattered dreams written on the faces of homesteaders who abandoned claims ruined by years of drought, grasshopper infestation, hailstorms, and falling prices. When desperation prompted them to move farther west or back to the Midwest where many had come from, they often left behind horses used for farm chores and transportation.

When set loose, the animals became semi-wild and survived as best they could off the land.

Those factors played into Jim's passion for horses.

"Whether it was to herd cattle or just be under the stars in Big Sky, Montana, Jim loved to ride." His father encouraged that impulse, telling Jim that living in Carterville meant that to get a new horse, "all a boy had to do was go into the hills where wild horses ran," catch one and break it.

Unlike Jim's grandparents, realists who learned how to survive in an unforgiving land, a wave of optimists flocked to the Treasure State in the early years of the 20th century, drawn by boosterism from officials of the transcontinental railroads that crossed the state. Promoters bombarded U.S. and foreign towns and cities with promises of bounteous harvests of wheat and other crops. Railroads would benefit from shipping those commodities to distant markets.

For a few years, the rains came, and farmers grew bumper crops. World War I, and the huge demand it created for foodstuffs and wool needed by soldiers, sailors and civilians, provided a market for all the crops and livestock that Montana could raise. Agriculture thrived, but peace came, and the market shrank. Drought followed, and during the 1920s, Montana suffered the largest population loss of any state.

Hard times hammered Eastern Montana farmers and ranchers in the 1930s. "Many of the smaller places just couldn't hold on, and either let their land go back to the county for taxes or sold out to the larger outfits," Bill Muri said. Prices for land in the "north country" dropped to 25 cents to 50 cents an acre, and farmers trying to hang on could barely pay taxes and the notes for loans on their land.

Destitution on a scale hard to imagine today spread all around Jim during the so-called "Dirty Thirties" — just as he pondered his life's calling. In neighboring Custer County, for example, stories of horses trying to survive on barren rangeland were still being told 70 years after the Great Depression.

Thus, when Jim announced that he didn't intend to become a farmer, he displayed reality about the dismal prospects of an agricultural living in Eastern Montana. If he could take to the sky and get paid for it, he could pursue his passion and likely escape from poverty.

Dreams, however, had to wait. Jim and his brothers needed to work hard and help their family of 11 make ends meet.

The older Muri brothers found jobs shoveling sugar beets during the fall harvest of this primary cash crop in several Eastern Montana counties. In the 1930s, before mechanized sugar beet harvesters, the harvest involved a series of manual tasks. A plow-like device pulled by a horse team lifted the beets from the ground. Laborers grabbed the beets by their leaves, shook them against each other to knock off soil and laid the large root vegetables single file in rows. Workers with beet hooks followed, grabbing the beets and chopping the crown and leaves from the root, and laborers with pitchforks tossed the beets into wagons or beds of early-model trucks.

The Muri boys' job was to shovel beets from wagons or trucks onto the ground at the beet dumps, where they awaited shipment by train to the Holly Sugar Co. factory in Sidney, Montana.

Sometimes the brothers had to miss high school to help with the sugar beet harvest at its peak. Bill, although fitted with an artificial leg because he lost the limb in an accident — a wagon wheel caught his leg when he was 4 — displayed toughness as he grew up. He could surpass any two men in shoveling beets, a younger brother, "Buck" Muri, said during a 2013 Memorial Day weekend conversation in Bill's Miles City home.

Skimpy pay barely rewarded the brothers' hard work. "You got so stiff you couldn't move," Bill said. The toughest time was at the start of a shift, when a teenage worker muscled his shovel into a pile of beets before he got warmed up. "Then you got so you could go fine," Bill Muri said.

Sugar beets provided a bright spot in the Rosebud County economy for a while. New irrigation projects completed along the Yellowstone River Valley — beets need more water than dryland farming staples such as wheat and oats — made the sugar industry viable. Sugar beets flourished for a while in Jim's adolescence. When he turned 13 in 1931, 71 train cars of beets left Carterville for the Holly factory, part of a total harvest from Rosebud County of 573 carloads, worth about $172,000 ($2.85 million in 2018 dollars). That economic boost, however, ended a few years later when Holly stopped buying beets from Carterville farmers, according to the *Billings* (MT) *Gazette* (December 24, 1931).

When Jim enrolled at CCHS, he joined Bill, two grades ahead of him, as an FFA member. Jim attended the district FFA convention in Billings during his sophomore year, and in April 1935, when he was a junior, Jim was among 16 youths awarded the state farmer degree — the highest award the Montana FFA offered — at the association's state convention, according to the *Great Falls Tribune* (April 27, 1935)

Yet, Bill Muri said his brother "never was much of a farmer. He wanted to get out and he did, in 1936."

Jim's grades earned him membership in the school's National Honor Society chapter, and he also excelled in athletics. As a 6-4 junior center, he played on the Cowboys' 1935 state high school basketball championship team, which defeated Great Falls, 28-20, in front of a then-record crowd of 3,000 in Havre. Jim also earned honorable mention honors on the all-state football team for his play at end, according to the *Helena* (MT) *Independent-Record* (December 4, 1935).

Jim starred in track, too; there, he passed an early test of his ability to think quickly and avoid danger. One day he was pole vaulting with a new birch pole. It broke as he crossed the bar, making him think for an instant he would impale himself. Somehow, he gyrated enough to avoid the sharp splintered end of the pole and fell uninjured to the ground. Jim placed fourth in pole vaulting at the state track meet in Missoula in May 1936, according to the *Montana Standard* (Butte, MT) (May 15, 1936).

Back in Miles City, Mary Johnson always had grandsons around to help with chores, but fun was not a stranger at her house. Jim proved to be a master at pulling good-natured pranks on his grandmother.

One evening, for example, Jim put a wolf pelt in her bed. Speaking to a woman friend at the house, "Grandma said, 'We've got a snake in the bed,'" Buck Muri said, chuckling at the memory.

Another time, basketball became the way to pull off a joke. Mary Johnson often heard Jim bang around in her kitchen in the evening, making himself a late meal after getting home from practice, but she had never been to a basketball game. Buck Muri said his grandmother told the boys she would like to watch a game, possibly because the Cowboys, with Jim on the roster, had become the toast of the town.

The Muri brothers made their grandmother "half embarrassed," Buck said, by telling her a fib: "Granny, I don't know if you want to go. They play naked, you know."

Buck laughed. "Oh, my god. She had a fit."

Frank Wiley influenced Jim Muri and other aspiring local aviators who reached high school age in the prewar years. Custer County High School, from which Wiley graduated in 1922 and which would award Muri his diploma in 1936, established the first aviation course in the state in 1930.

Wiley supervised the program. Muri was too young to be in the class then — he turned 12 that year — but his chance would come.

When the class was first offered, high school students and interested adults met twice a week for two-hour "recitation periods." The course encompassed study in four areas:

1. Aerodynamics and the theory of flight.
2. Airplane construction and U.S. Department of Commerce regulations and air traffic rules.
3. Airplane motors.
4. Meteorology and navigation.

The course featured lectures by "prominent professional men and noted pilots." Students practiced rigging the latest planes. Lessons focused on satisfying growing demand by budding pilots for "an organized ground school course of study and to acquaint them with the basic principles of aviation."

Jim's ambition to become a pilot might have increased during his junior year in high school when he got to see a group of Army Air Corps planes fly into Miles City. Perhaps he got a chance to talk to pilots and crew members.

The opportunity came when the War Department converted 18 planes into "snowmushers" to use in field training flights over the Northwest. The flights in January and February 1935 tested planes and personnel under subzero conditions during flights over an area between Duluth, Minnesota, and Great Falls, Montana.

The squadron, down to thirteen planes, left Billings and flew to Miles City on February 19, 1935. It comprised three P-12K Boeing pursuits, two A-12 Curtiss attack planes, four Douglas observation planes and two Martin bombers, according to the *Miles City Star* (February 20, 1935).

En route to Miles City, the Douglas planes flew over the Little Big Horn battlefield in a symbolic salute to those who died there. Miles City rolled out the welcome mat to the fliers and ground crews. Officers dined at the landmark Miles City Club, enlisted men at the Elks Lodge, and dancing capped the evening at both places.

The next day, the so-called "Arctic Patrol" left Miles City, and on February 20, it reached Bismarck, North Dakota.

The following school year (1935-36), when Muri was a senior, he took the aviation course, renamed aeronautics, which had been incorporated into the daily educational schedule. Joseph "J.E." Mutchler, a mathematics teacher, was the original instructor and continued to teach the class. Students learned the history of aviation, aerodynamics, aircraft rules and regulations, materials and construction of airplanes, aviation, meteorology and "ground rules." Jim was among twenty-six boys who took the class, which emphasized material that student pilots would have to master to pass the federal government's exam and earn their pilot's licenses.

Instruction included a step-by-step guide to building a model airplane. Along with weather maps, the guide contained questions and answers that helped a novice pilot learn the basics of an aircraft's assembly, navigation, compass work, and how to follow a heading in flight. The teacher asked students to list the 10 materials used in aircraft construction, and they got to simulate building historic planes by constructing models of early planes, such as a Wright biplane and a Curtiss "June Bug."

When Jim wasn't thinking about sports, or his high school classes, or coming up with a good way to josh his grandmother, his mind was on flying and following the feats of his best friend.

Hank Swartz took flying lessons at the Miles City airport while in high school. Jim's parents couldn't afford that, but the future B-26 pilot got a vicarious flight experience. He'd pay 60 cents to ride the Milwaukee train from Carterville to Miles City so he could watch Swartz fly.

Swartz completed flying lessons and earned his student pilot's license on January 7, 1936. Two teenagers, Hank and Jim, were ready to shed that stage of their lives.

For Jim, the days of cowboying in Carterville and growing up under the eyes of his grandmother in Miles City were coming to a close. Graduation neared. He envisioned young adult life, with it challenges and accomplishments. He was confident he and Hank would become airplane pilots. They moved closer to that goal in May 1936.

Chapter 3 - Taking after Hank

Almost 1,000 people packed the Custer County High School gymnasium on a warm Thursday, May 28, 1936, in Miles City, according to the *Miles City Star* (May 29, 1936). Family members, friends and others awaited commencement for 142 graduates, half boys, half girls, who gathered outside the gym.

"Can you believe it? We're done!" Jim Muri said to Hank Swartz as the pair and their classmates awaited instructions to march inside for the commencement ceremony. It got prominent display in the *Star* (May 29, 1936)

"What are you gonna do now?" a classmate asked Muri.

"I want to be an airplane pilot. I want to fly," he replied. Hank nodded. He and Jim took the CCHS aviation class together; a photo of the class in the school yearbook shows them standing next to each other. Swartz already had gained experience as a pilot through flying lessons he took during high school at the Miles City airport. Seeing his friend at the controls of a plane and then watching him take off further fueled Jim's ambitions to find adventure in the air.

Just then, the high school orchestra played the Pomp and Circumstance march, and a faculty member signaled the graduates it was time to enter the gym.

"Finally! We did it!" Excited murmurs rippled through the gray-robe-clad group, mortar boards perched on their heads, tassels on their left. Girls and boys met at the center aisle and marched in pairs to their seats. Proud faculty members took seats behind the class.

The seniors recognized at least three, maybe four, of the dignitaries present for their big night: The Rev. J.L. Craig, who gave the invocation; Principal R.H. Wollin; R.H. Michaels, president of the school board; and possibly Montana Governor Elmer Holt. G. Ott Romney, athletic director at Brigham Young University, gave the commencement speech.

Romney advised the graduates to think of life as a series of commencements, each the attainment of a personal goal someone set, which would become a starting place for another milestone.

He advised the high schoolers to look at the world of science where opportunities awaited them in airplanes and flight, radio, surgery and medicine, engineering and other fields. The mention of aviation made Muri and Swartz think the speaker was talking to them. They weren't sure what the future held, but they sensed that their dream of getting pilots' wings could become real. We'll soar far from Miles City, they told themselves.

Romney told the students to never forget their spiritual side in a materialistic world, suggesting lessons found in the life of George C. Calnan, who represented the United States as a fencer at the 1932 Olympics in Los Angeles. Games officials chose Calnan, a young Navy lieutenant, to take the Olympic oath on behalf of athletes from 47 countries as the Games began. A year later, he was one of 73 people killed in the crash of the USS Akron, a helium-filled rigid airship, off the New Jersey coast.

Romney asked the graduates to imagine Lieutenant Calnan standing at his post aboard the airship just before it crashed and recommended building "happy memory books." When you review your life in the years ahead, the "books" will help you remember adventures that will stay with you until death, he said.

OK, Muri thought, but I hope they give us our diplomas soon. Life is waiting.

After two more musical selections, Governor Holt, an 1899 graduate of the school, greeted the graduates. "Go through life considering the rights of others," he said, "and at all times be a square shooter."

After more ceremonial matters, school administrators awarded scholarships for use at the Montana university system, and then the most-awaited time of the night came. Muri strode across the stage, shook Wollin's hand and received his diploma, signifying completion of vocational agriculture coursework. A few minutes later, the principal presented Swartz with his diploma, which formalized his achievement on the academic track.

What's next? Big things, we hope, Muri and Swartz told themselves.

Possibly Jim and Hank saw an Army recruiting poster in the post office or another public building. That spurred their decision to join the military and pursue their goal of becoming Air Corps pilots.

"Let's sign up. Maybe the Army will send us to the same place for training," Jim said. Hank nodded in agreement.

They both sensed adventures ahead.

Hank, being older, was eligible to sign up in the summer of 1936 and may have done so at his earliest opportunity. Jim, however, didn't turn 18 until October that year, so he had to wait.

Hank got his Army orders first. He reported to Chanute Field in Illinois, where he learned welding, sheet metal fabrication and related skills. Jim followed him to the Midwestern base about a month later.

45

The Army sent Swartz to Hamilton Field, in the northern California city of Novato, where he became a cadet in the bombardment squadron. He stayed at the base until 1939.

More education seemed the way to further his career prospects, so Swartz enrolled in a tool engineering course at Marin Junior College. While a student, he worked for Douglas Aircraft Co. According to a *Miles City Star* article (no date), he entered the "senior unit" of UCLA and earned an Associate of Arts degree on June 2, 1940. He became an Air Corps assistant aircraft inspector at March Field and began advanced training at Mather Field in March 1941. He graduated from that program on October 30, 1941 and received a commission as an Air Corps officer. The Corps assigned him to duty in the Philippines as a military bombardment and transport pilot.

Swartz frequently thought about his Miles City buddy. In a June 8, 1941, letter to his family, while he was a member of the Flying Cadets at California's Moffett Field, he said:

"Jim Muri is now a Lieutenant; he has been transferred to Langley Field, Virginia. That is really a good field. I'm hoping I can get transferred there, too. If not there, maybe I can get to Salt Lake City. I have plenty of time to worry about that, though. Right now, I have to worry about graduating and getting my commission."

The friendship between Swartz and Muri continued when the Army sent both to California, Swartz to the north in the San Francisco area and Muri to the south at locations near Los Angeles. After getting to the Golden State, Swartz met and married a woman from Sacramento.

Hank met and was fond of Alice Moyer, his friend's girlfriend and soon-to-be wife. He wrote her on letterhead from a San

Francisco hotel on November 21, 1941. The letter, addressed to "My Dear Little Alice Blue Gown," said Hank hoped she had received a picture of him, intended for her and Jim, and continued, "I have a lot of news for you, so I will tell you in a hurry and get it over with.

"First of all, I am a married man. I fell in love with Edna Peterson, a very nice blonde girl and I love her very much. Second, I got sent to the Philippines Islands, but I will try to get back when they let me. In the meantime, I will whip the Japs for recreation," he said.

Hank also wrote Jim, who would be "very surprised" to hear the "good news" of Swartz's overseas deployment. Big changes were in the air for the two Montana guys, and they and millions of Americans would undergo a life-shaping upheaval in less than three weeks when the Japanese attacked Pearl Harbor.

Perhaps sensing how transitory personal relationships could be with war looming, Swartz offered advice. "You two had better get married or I am going to be very angry with both of you. Take it from me – there's nothing like married life."

Weeks later, on December 23, 1941, Hank also wrote his family on Schmalze Street in Miles City, saying little because of wartime censorship.

"About all I can tell you is I am in a place where we don't have to worry about the enemy at all. I am very disappointed because we won't be able to get into any combat until March at the earliest. We are all very anxious to get a crack at the dirty slant eyes," he said.

In what would prove to be bitter irony, Hank tried to reassure his family he'd be all right.

"Don't believe any rumors about me being lost or anything. I know that you won't hear from me for long periods of time but that means I am okay. It certainly is true that no news is good news.

"Please don't worry about me, folks. I am quite happy and getting along exceptionally well."

An A-24 rolled off the Douglas Aircraft Co. production line in the fall of 1941. It was the Army Air Corps' version of the Navy Dauntless dive-bomber; the Army took delivery of the plane at Savannah, Georgia, on October 21, 1941. It joined "Project X" on January 2, 1942, and six days later, mechanics disassembled the plane and shipped it overseas to "Sumac," the code name for Australia. The Army assigned an A-24, carrying serial number 41-15798, to the 5th Air Force, 3rd Bombardment Group, 8th Bombardment Squadron, Hank's unit, and it became his plane on his last mission.

News about Swartz got back to his hometown through a report in the *Miles City Star* (no date) in the spring of 1942. The brief item said his parents received word that the Air Force had sent Hank's unit to Australia.

"Henry writes that he is getting along fine and would like to hear from his Miles City friends," the article said, listing Swartz's San Francisco APO address. Letters "must not show his rank nor bear a return address," the *Star* said. It quoted Swartz as saying he could write letters on one side of paper "but twice a week."

Jim and Hank both passed through Hickam Field, so it's possible they were in Hawaii at the same time for a few weeks in February and March 1942. Then, the Army Air Force sent Hank into combat in the southwest Pacific. Sylvia Saadati said during phone calls in the spring of 2019 that she heard her father tried to find his Miles City buddy on the sprawling military base during the brief window of opportunity. Jim's efforts didn't succeed.

Hank Swartz began a diary at the start of 1942. He recorded what he saw most days, brief impressions from a Montanan sent halfway around the world by a country at war.

Easter fell on April 5th in 1942, when Hank was at Port Moresby, the capital of New Guinea. The next day, he wrote an informative diary entry:

"Port Moresby - (Kela Kela) a lot of B-26s, P-39s and P-40s and B-17s came in last night. Six B-24(s) came in this morning. We started on our raid at 11 o'clock. The Japs hit us (as) we were circling the field. We got away. The P-40s and P-39s shot down a few. When we landed again, we found the Japs had done no damage. They shot down two P-40s, but the pilots are okay."

The B-26s Swartz saw were part of Muri's unit, the 22nd Bomb Group. By then, ships had had carried many B-26s to Hawaii where mechanics reassembled them, and the Corps assigned pilots and crews to the bombers. In groups of three, the B-26s left for Australia to help in the vital defense of the island continent against an expected Japanese thrust into the Southwest Pacific. In a twist of fate, Muri, who hoped to see his hometown buddy again in the Pacific front, didn't get the chance because the Air Corps held Muri and another 22nd group pilot, Herb Mayes, at Hickam Field for a future mission that was a mystery to them.

The 22nd made its combat debut on April 5, 1942, when Marauders, based in Townsville, bombed Japan's New Guinea stronghold of Rabaul. Admiral Nimitz's official record of 1942 action in the Pacific confirms what Swartz saw and recorded in his diary.

"One B-17 attacked the Rabaul airdrome and six B-26 [first appearance] bombed the shipping in that harbor with fair success," according to Nimitz's so-called *Graybook*.

Hank, by now a second lieutenant, got orders to take off from a New Guinea airstrip, the start of his first combat mission, on April 6. He and his gunner, Sgt. John J. Stephenson, climbed into their dive bomber and flew off with three other A-24s from 7-Mile Drome near Port Moresby on a mission against the Japanese stronghold at Lae, on the opposite side of New Guinea with the Stanley Range dividing Japanese-held and Allied-held parts of the massive island.

Halfway around the world from his hometown of Miles City, Hank flew on his mission with someone with Eastern Montana roots. Stephenson was born in Forsyth, Montana, graduated from high school in Billings and attended Montana State University in Missoula (now the University of Montana).

Six P-40E Kitty Hawks from the Royal Australian Air Force's 75th Squadron escorted the A-24s. First Lieutenant Roger G. Ruegg led the A-24s in place of Commanding Officer Floyd "Buck" Rogers, sidelined with dengue fever.

The Americans reached their target, and the A-24s barreled downward to attack. Swartz's plane was last seen diving toward an anti-aircraft gun position. What happened next remains a mystery. None of the Allied fliers, including those in Ruegg's formation, saw Swartz's plane go down or crash. It's believed Zero fighters intercepted and shot down the dive bomber.

Military officials declared Swartz missing in action on April 7, 1942. Later that month, his parents received a telegram at their Miles City home from Major Gen. James Alexander Union, telling them about Hank's MIA status.

B-26 attacks on Rabaul continued until May 27, 1942; they resulted in the loss of seven bombers. After that, the Army Air Force used B-25 Mitchell bombers to attack Rabaul, and Townsville-based B-26s from the 22nd carried out missions against Lae.

In the summer of 1942, a reporter from the hometown *Miles City Star* interviewed Swartz's parents a few months after he went missing. Although they had received the Army telegram by then, his mother said she and her husband "still have hope that Henry will be reported among those still in active duty," adding that she sensed he would return home.

"Why, look here," she said, holding a clipping from the *Seattle Times*. "Henry was among a number of soldiers who were awarded a Silver Star — that was in last June (1942). He was in Melbourne, Australia, because the story was written from that city."

The article said General George H. Brett, Allied Air Commander in the Southwest Pacific presented 17 Silver Stars to "heroic American airmen" and twelve pilots were cited for "successful bombing raids on Japanese airdromes."

Hank's father, H.G. Swartz, a Milwaukee Railroad worker, said the military told him and his wife their son was missing after the Lae mission. "And then we received the clipping from friends who took it out of a Seattle newspaper, and mother here wrote it out word for word, and that was in June, around the 10th as I remember.

"Wouldn't you think from that, our telegram from Ulio (that) our son was reported in missing in action, and then in June reading that story about Henry getting a Silver Star for heroic action —

that he might still be somewhere ... alive?" the senior Swartz said.

It wasn't just his parents who clung to hope that Hank Swartz had survived and might await rescue somewhere in the Pacific. His wife, Edna, pregnant and living in her hometown of Sacramento, voiced the same sentiment in a June 1, 1942, letter to her Montana in-laws.

"How much longer do you think we will have to wait before we hear from Hank?" she asked, adding that her father dreamed a few nights earlier that "Hank came home, and he said it was so real, it woke him up. If we could just know that he is well and getting what he needs to eat, but the uncertainty is so hard to bear."

The government declared Swartz and Stephenson dead after the war in the Pacific ended, Swartz on December 19, 1945, and Stephenson on November 19 of that year. Their country honored the Montanans by having their names placed on the tablets of the missing at the Manilla American Cemetery.

The A-24's record in the Pacific includes brief service in the Java and New Guinea theaters with the 3rd Third Bomb Group. Devasting losses to Zero fighters prompted the Air Force to withdraw the Third from combat at the end of July.

When Hank went missing in New Guinea, his fate affected more than his family and friends back home, his young wife, and Jim, his best friend since they were high school classmates in Miles City. Hank and Jim's close relationship became a three-way bond just before the U.S. entered World War II when the Army Air Corps sent the pair to California, Jim to the Los Angeles area in the south and Hank to the northern part of the state. In their new surroundings, the Montanans' orbit grew to include Alice Moyer, the Riverside woman who became Jim's girlfriend, then fiancé, and wife in late December 1941.

Jim and Alice didn't meet Hank's wife, Edna, before the Air Corps sent Hank to the Philippines in November 1941, according to what Sylvia Saadati heard later from her parents. Hank, however, made his fondness for Alice clear in his greetings to her that month. Besides "My Dear Little Alice Blue Gown" on the November 21 letter from San Francisco, Hank wrote to "My Dear Little Blue Eyes" in a postcard mailed from the Philippines on November 28.

Thus, it came as a shock to Jim, in Hawaii, and Alice, in Riverside, when they got word that Hank and his crewman, John Stephenson, were missing in action on a mission against the Japanese above New Guinea in April 1942. Jim and Alice expressed sadness at the news — and their hope that Hank had survived — in letters written that spring, but they apparently didn't survive the passage of time.

Yet there's no doubt that the news of Hank's ill-fated mission hit Jim and Alice hard.

In an April 2019 Facebook message, Sylvia said her father knew Hank was missing by the time Jim reached Midway on May 29, 1942, six days before his harrowing mission, "but he was convinced that [Hank] was just down in the jungle, like some others, and would be found."

After Midway, Sylvia said, Alice and Jim thought Hank might have come walking out of the jungle, perhaps in the Philippines, after his final mission. That unfounded hope arose from a letter Alice got from her in-laws, who passed on erroneous information drawn from the dream Hank's father-in-law had. Edna's father shared his thoughts with Hank's family in Miles City, who mentioned them to the Eastern Montana Muris.

Sylvia said she's heard of a letter her father sent her mother soon after his narrow escape from death at Midway, in which Jim assured Alice he was doing all he could to find Hank and was sure he would succeed.

"It was better they didn't know for sure right after Midway as Dad was suffering from the loss of his other close friends and having nightmares once he managed to sleep. No Montana boy could have been prepared for what he experienced," Sylvia said.

Chapter 4 - Training Time

After Jim enlisted in the Army Air Corps in the fall of 1936, he received orders to report to a base more than 1,000 miles from his home in Eastern Montana. On December 11, 1936, he arrived at Chanute Field in Rantoul, Illinois, downstate near Champaign-Urbana. The base, about 20 years old, was established in 1917 as one of 32 Air Service training camps created after the U.S. entered World War I. It got its name from Octave Chanute, an early aeronautical engineer and experimenter, and a friend and adviser to the Wright brothers. Until 1938, it provided all the technical training for the Air Corps.

Assigned the rank of Private AM 2c1, Jim began his study of welding and airplane engine mechanics. All around him, the base began a rapid growth spurt after being spared Washington's budget axe. Influential Illinois congressmen, including legendary Republican Everett Dirksen, had fended off attempts to transfer Chanute's technical school to Denver.

By Christmas 1936, Jim Muri seemed to have adjusted well to his new life in the Army Air Corps. On December 22 that year, he mailed greetings to his father back home in Carterville.

"Just sending cards to show what is going on here every day," he wrote on a postcard with a photo of Chanute Airfield on the opposite side.

"I like it swell and I'm having a good time as well," he said.

It didn't take long for Jim to strike up a friendship at the base with someone whose socioeconomic background was similar to his. A picture taken in December 1936 shows a pair of teenagers dressed in coveralls, typical work clothing for those who shoveled coal to keep Chanute's heating plant running. The caption on the picture says: "Jim Muri, A Rancher/Farmer's son from Miles City, Montana" and "Joseph T. Diviak, A Coalminer's son from Caretta, WV." The men stayed in touch over the decades and reunited almost seven decades later when Muri, by then a long-retired U.S. Air Force lieutenant colonel, received the Jimmy Doolittle Award at Arlington, Virginia.

A document titled "Old Buddies" includes the 1936 photo and one taken in November 2003 at the Doolittle event. It shows Muri standing next to Diviak, retired after nine years with the Army Air Corps/Army Air Force and 27 years as a civil service employee of the Air Force.

By late 1939, Chanute spread over 950 acres and was home to the largest school of its kind in the world, according to the *Chicago Daily Tribune* (December 22, 1939). The Air Corps announced a goal of training 13,000 aviation mechanics and radio operators by 1941 to fill a need for crewmen with tactical squadrons expected to fly 5,500 military planes by 1944.

Between buildings and equipment under construction or planned in late 1939, Chanute expected $14 million in improvements. That would make it "one of the most important posts" in the U.S.'s expanding air force. Colonel Davenport Johnson, a veteran army flyer, commanded a staff of 80 officers who taught Chanute students, the *Tribune* said.

To see Chanute, which resembled a well-planned large city, after his years surrounded by Miles City's cowboy town ambience, must have given Jim pause. At the landing field, runways were being built that would require enough concrete to make 32 miles of an 18-foot highway. New barracks that cost $1.8 million housed 2,200 men, and a pair of $800,000 buildings for the radio mechanics schools were under construction; each contained a flight hanger the size of a football field.

The Army was building a central heating plant and homes for commissioned and noncommissioned officers. Corpsmen who needed medical care — a flu outbreak sickened 54 officers and enlisted men in early January 1937, according to the *Decatur* (IL) *Herald* (January 16, 1937) — got care at a new 120-bed hospital. The base also boasted a golf course, a swimming pool and tennis courts.

Muri arrived at Chanute in 1936, but he likely experienced the same or similar break-in routine as recruits in 1939 did. They started with three weeks of drills and army discipline followed by a month of basic training that covered mathematics, air corps fundamentals and the principles of electricity and machinery. Then came five months in the technical school. When a student graduated, the Army assigned him to a squadron at one of the Chanute fields.

Students got a mix of theory and practical experience in their training. One class, taught in a hangar, allowed the men to work with P-36 Curtiss pursuit planes. They got to tear down and rebuild the planes, and they helped test the planes by flying them with army pilots.

When Jim finished his time at Chanute, the Air Corps sent him to Southern California for the next phase of his training. He finished two years of study in aviation-related subjects at Riverside City College while stationed at nearby March Field as a Flying Cadet. He trained in planes such as the Stearman PT-13 and the Douglas C-29, but then his attention wandered from aviation.

A friend set him up on a blind date with Alice Moyer, of

Riverside, California. It was May of 1940. Alice was about two months away from her 19th birthday, on July 17.

Alice was born in Roseburg, Oregon. Both of her parents — father Ralph and mother Anne — grew up in Riverside, where they were childhood sweethearts. Ralph lost an arm in a sawing accident and took his young family to Oregon, where he worked on a well-known nursery owned by his uncle, Clarence Moyer. The thought that one of her small children might fall into a deep creek running through Clarence Moyer's orchard terrified Anne, so the family returned to Riverside.

Ralph Moyer became the city constable and sang in the local opera. Alice barely knew her father, who died when she was 5 from blood poisoning, the result of in-office surgery. This left his wife a widow with four children just before the Great Depression began. Anne Moyer "made ends meet while her kids were little," her granddaughter Sylvia Saadati said, by raising rabbits, chickens and roosters; taking in laundry; ironing clothes; and putting her skills as an accomplished seamstress to use.

When Alice entered the workforce, she held a variety of jobs. The position she held longest was as secretary to the president of Bank of America's Riverside branch (*Big Timber*, MT, *Pioneer*, June 26, 2001). "She did a little bit of everything; she was a good employee and had a lot of responsibility," Saadati said of her mother.

When Jim met Alice, he wasn't meeting someone sight unseen. Soon after the go-between arranged the date but before it took place, Jim was in Riverside, and a friend or acquaintance pointed Alice out to him. The tall Montanan said to himself, I want to meet that girl.

That desired event occurred a couple days later. Jim drove his car to Alice's mother's house on Hillcrest Avenue to pick her up. He saw a dark-haired beauty waiting for him. Sylvia related that she'd heard he "had his breath knocked out" when he first met Alice.

Alice wore a beautiful blue dress. She cocked her eyebrow and smiled at Jim, and he was tongue-tied the rest of the night. They drove to their first date, perhaps doing something traditional for young adults of that era such as heading to the soda counter of the local five-and-dime Woolworth's store.

The first date over, the ice broken, Jim and Alice found conversation becoming easier. Something clicked between the ranch kid who came from a hardscrabble background in Montana and the girl who had returned to Southern California after a stay in Oregon and who also knew about hard times. Jim became comfortable enough to ask Alice if she had a nickname and, learning she didn't, he asked if it was all right for him to give her one since he had one. Those in his circle called him The Hammer "because he got things done."

Jim told Alice he'd like to call her *Susie-Q*. And that was OK with her.

Where did "Susie-Q" come from? No one can say for sure. Perhaps Jim was thinking of a step that became popular in the 1930s in such dances as the Big Apple, Lindy, Hop and others. The step originated from a novelty dance, which derived from a 1936 song, "Doin' the Suzie-Q," composed by Tennessee native Lil Hardin Armstrong, the second wife of Louis Armstrong.

Radio swept across America in the 1920s and 1930s and had become an influential medium by the 1940s, so maybe Jim heard the song on the airwaves. Or, maybe he and Alice found a club in the Los Angeles area where they could swing on out and do the "Suzie-Q."

Although those theories sound plausible, neither of Jim and Alice Muri's children, James and Sylvia, embrace them. Sylvia said her father, like many young people of the time, had little or no exposure to minorities or minority culture before he entered the armed forces. She said he expressed bigoted sentiments in her presence as she was growing up. Yet, Jim Muri's attitudes toward people of color were common in the America of the 1940s, 1950s and even 1960s.

Whatever the origin, the *Susie-Q* nickname stuck. If the Muris needed any reminder of the enduring popularity of Alice's moniker, all they had to do was listen to the radio in the late 1950s, when Dale Hawkins' rockabilly version hit Billboard magazine's Top 100 chart. Much changed, "Susie-Q" became a signature hit for Credence Clearwater Revival after the rock group released it as a single in 1968. Jim and Alice probably weren't rock 'n' roll fans, but they and their friends had children who grew up in the 1960s and 1970s. Those young people might have honored a hero of Midway by humming a song that put a smile on his face because it reminded him of his wife.

The relationship blossomed, and Alice accepted Jim's proposal of marriage. The engaged couple were a continent apart, Jim on the East Coast and Alice on the West Coast, in the summer of 1941. They kept in touch through regular letter-writing.

Chapter 5 - Ready for war

Jim's career progressed as 1941 began. Sent to Texas by the Air Corps, he shared good news about his latest step up the flight ladder with Alice in Riverside and his family in Montana.

"They've assigned me to Randolph Field," he told them. That name carried cachet in the 1930s and 1940s. Dedicated in 1930, the base, about 15 miles northeast of San Antonio, became known as the "West Point of the Air" — the name of a 1935 movie shot at Randolph — and the "Showplace of the Air Force," according to a *Houston Chronicle* blog piece about the base's 80th birthday (June 20, 2010).

From January 6 until March 14, 1941, Jim logged hours flying a primary trainer and a bomber trainer. News of his accomplishments got back to Montana; Butte's *Montana Standard* (March 18, 1941), reported that Muri and a Butte man, R. Bourne MacDonald, were members of the largest class, 410 fledgling airmen, to ever graduate from Randolph's basic training school.

Both Montanans transitioned to nearby Kelly Field next to complete a combined 30 weeks of flight instruction there and at Randolph.

At Kelly, his base from March 17-May 29, Jim moved up to a BC-1, which gave him experience in a plane with a retractable tailwheel landing gear, provision for armament and a two-way radio. A 550-hp engine furnished power.

The BC-1, also known as the North American T-6 Texan, was an advanced single-engine trainer used by the USAAF, Navy, the Royal Air Force and other British Commonwealth Air Forces to instruct pilots during World War II. The modern U.S. Air Force used the T-6 into the 1970s.

Jim graduated from Kelly on May 29, 1941 and received his pilot rating. No longer a Flying Cadet, he now was a Second Lieutenant, an Army officer among the 12,000 men accepted into the Air Corps in 1941.

June 1941 found Jim training in a Martin B-14, which used the airframe of the B-10, the first all-metal monoplane bomber put in service by the Air Corps. Pilots who flew the B-10 and planes based on it considered this series of bombers superior to Army pursuit aircraft they had flown.

When the B-10 came out in 1934, General Henry "Hap" Arnold called it a revolutionary development in military aircraft because it could fly 50 percent faster than any biplane bomber, and it also could outrun fighters of the time. This Martin bomber made other bombers obsolete in the view of air power experts.

By July 1941, Jim was on the East Coast at Langley Field near Washington, D.C. He continued flying BT-14s and added experience at the controls of a Douglas bomber, the B-18 Bolo. This medium bomber, designed to replace the B-10, tarnished the reputation of the U.S. aircraft industry. By 1940, only three years after the Air Corps accepted it, the Bolo was underpowered with inadequate defensive armament and able to carry only a small bomb load. Japanese attacks against Pearl Harbor and the Philippines in December 1941 destroyed many B-18s.

In September 1941, Jim and the rest of the 22nd joined the famed Louisiana maneuvers, which were a series of major U.S. Army exercises that took place in northern and western Louisiana. About 400,000 troops took part in the exercises, which tested U.S. training, logistics, doctrine and commanders. The group got new B-25s in July, and Jim and other pilots flew the Mitchells to

Ellington Field, Texas, which was their base during the exercise. The 22nd members were part of the Blue Army during the maneuvers.

For some of the airmen, Texas presented an alien vast blank space. It seemed less forbidding to Muri as someone who had grown up in Montana's Big Open country. Still, the simulated battle required change by all.

Chatting among themselves, Jim and his colleagues said the imaginary bombs they were carrying on their planes were a stretch from the real deal. "We look for enemy tanks, drop bombs," they said, and then, as Bob Leonard of the 18th Recon squadron put it, "We erased the slate except for the 10 best targets." Later, after combat experience, he would say that "it sure turned out to be a different world when there was a real war declared and we started using real bombs that could only be used one time."

Crews often ate meals on a hit-and-miss basis. Limited mess hall hours meant that airmen were frequently airborne over Louisiana when cooks served chow. They worked up appetites — one crew, for example, logged 110 hours of flight time in 10 days.

Some of the 22nd fliers — it's unknown if Jim was among them — might have gotten their first look at B-26s during the maneuvers. Thirteen B-26s from Patterson Field in Ohio flew to Ellington on September 6 and took part on the side of General Walter Krueger, the Blue Force commander.

The B-26 had been rolling off the lines at the Glenn Martin Co. plant in Baltimore for about a year then, but Jim would have to wait about a month to get a close look at the much-heralded bomber that would bring him fame.

Partway through the maneuvers, Major General H.A. Darque

spoke to the press from Lake Charles, Louisiana. He praised the safety tactics of the 800 pilots who flew in the war games, among them Muri, according to the *Washington* (DC) *Evening Star*.

New bombers were coming online in a rush to beef up U.S. air defenses, and those flown in the maneuvers performed well in their first field test, Darque said.

The B-26 got special praise. Quoted in the *Evening Star*, Robert A. Lovett, undersecretary in charge of air matters in the War Department, described the Martin Marauder as the fastest plane in the world, capable of flying more than 350 mph, according to Army fliers.

Gen. Darque commanded the Third Army in the maneuvers, which simulated combat with the Second Army. Each army received 400 planes.

"These maneuvers have been a test of new equipment of the most powerful type and highest speed we have had in our air force. It has been handled superbly by the pilots, but it is highly significant it has withstood the grueling test that has shown its worth," Darque said.

His 30-day stint in Louisiana over, Muri didn't wait long to get his break, the opportunity to fly a B-26. When the maneuvers ended, the Army sent him to San Antonio, Texas, to pick up a damaged plane that had been repaired.

"And when I returned to Langley, the organization as a whole had converted to the B-26 — B-25s were being phased out and the B-26s came in — and there were B-26s setting everywhere on the ramp on Langley Field," Muri recalled in a 1990 interview.

A friend, Lieutenant Mike Michaelis, approached Muri.

"Let me introduce you to your new plane," Michaelis said. He pointed to an "old" clipped-wing B-26 with a tail number 13 parked amid the other B-26s on the ramp.

Michaelis and Muri crawled into the cockpit, and the ranking officer gave directions.

"Now here's the way you start it," Michaelis said, showing Muri the procedure for starting the plane. Someone assigned Muri a co-pilot, and Michaelis continued his instructions.

"There's two or three things you should remember about the airplane. No. 1, it's all electric, so if you have trouble on takeoff, you must throw this switch and this switch," Michaelis said, motioning toward the controls. He gave more instructions, then offered a key pointer.

"Your approach speed should not be under 150 mph — so go fly it."

Muri was in for a new experience on his first B-26 flight, when he learned how different it was from the bomber he flew before.

"We went around the traffic pattern and the airplane didn't fly like the B-25 flew — it had a way of flying on its own. And we came in at 150 mph, a lot of speed, and we couldn't ... hold the altitude on the final approach like you would in a B-25."

Thanks to "a lot of good luck," Muri cleared some trees and landed his plane. Back on the ground, it was time to inspect the B-26 to better understand its workings.

"Well, we got all the people together and through classes and a lot of 'ifs' and 'ands' and 'buts,' we all decided how to fly the machine," he said.

That was the start of "real good luck" with B-26s for Muri and his fellow pilots.

November 1941 turned out to be a momentous month for the

22nd Bomb Group and Jim, one of its pilots. Early in the month, the group got orders to fly to Savannah, Georgia, to take part in the Carolina maneuvers. The 22nd's time in the exercise, however, lasted only a week before the Army cancelled the drills and ordered the squadron back to Langley Field.

Tom Calderwood, a 33rd Squadron parachute rigger, provided a vivid although confusing recollection of that time.

"The day before I was to leave (Georgia), I was checked out as a truck driver and drove to Savannah. I learned to drive the truck on the way. If someone would (have explained) to me why we were jerked out of those maneuvers in the middle of them and ordered back to Langley to install armor plate in the planes, I could believe that the powers in charge didn't know what was coming and couldn't have avoided Pearl Harbor."

Jim's flight log shows him with time at the controls of a Savannah-based B-26 on November 2 and 3, 1941. Then he confronted a serious health problem, aggravated by the fact he was a 23-year-old placed in unfamiliar surroundings about two thousand miles away from his Montana home and about the same distance away from his fiancé in Southern California. In a November 4, 1941, letter to Alice, written on Savannah Air Base stationery, he said, "Not much tonight, honey. I've got what is commonly called appendicitis. Not too bad but very distressing to say the least."

Muri said he hoped to be OK by the next day but for now the base commander had grounded him. He planned to "take it easy and absorb some of this Georgia sunshine." He termed the weather "wonderful," although it was "cold as hell" at night. Jim said he froze the night before when the men shared a blanket.

"I'm sure you would have been a valuable asset to (provide warmth) …, Alice — yes, yes," Jim said.

Now a five-year veteran of military life and barracks, Muri was ready for his next night in the South. "You can bet your sweet life I'll be warm. I mean with blankets."

Muri told his sweetheart he sampled "the famous Southern metropolis (Savannah)" the night before. "I can't say I like it. It's dark down there and very dirty and unkept. Not at all what I had expected to see."

After a seven-day layoff, Muri took to the air again. He flew 24 more times in November, four times as co-pilot and the remaining 20 as pilot. Meanwhile, as the countdown to war continued, Muri, his fellow 22nd pilots and crewmen and members of other Army Air Force squadrons felt the effects of major forces swirling around them, though they did not understand what was happening. A sense of impending conflict comes from an account given decades later by 2nd Lt. Lewis "Tad" Ford, a 33rd Squadron pilot.

"The November 12, 1941, so-called 'Icelandic Message' to GHQ (General Headquarters), which was located at Langley Field, was a military message, the essence of which was that 'this is it — prepare.' This kicked off an intensive training program involving dividing the 24-hour day into six four-hour periods," he said.

"We were assigned to something every four hours: fly, do bombing, gunnery, shoot skeet, take Link training, go to ground school. We were also assigned four-hour periods to sleep. Seldom did we get two (sleep breaks) together," he continued.

"So, when December 7th came, I got my first day off in a month."

Continuing, Lewis said the Army assigned airmen days off on a crew-by-crew basis and when he and his copilot had days off, the copilot had his own plans for relaxation. On his day off, Lewis slept late, "floated into town" and watched *Sergeant York* at the local theater.

"I was surprised about halfway through the picture to see my name come up on a caption underneath the movie, saying, 'Lieutenant Ford, report to the box office.' A driver was waiting for me with a staff car to give me a ride back to Langley Field. Pearl Harbor had happened."

Japan attacked Pearl Harbor with 353 warplanes launched from six aircraft carriers. Bombs and torpedoes damaged all eight U.S. Navy battleships tied up there and sank four of them. Japanese weaponry damaged or sank eight other ships and destroyed 188 aircraft. Overall, 2,403 Americans were killed, and 1,178 were wounded.

Jim Muri went to, or already was at, Langley Field on December 7, 1941, which President Franklin Roosevelt would call "a day of infamy" when he asked Congress to declare war against Japan. Congress passed the declaration by an 82-0 vote in the Senate and by a 388-1 margin in the house, the only dissenting vote cast by Montana representative Jeanette Rankin.

Chapter 6 – First Casualties

Peacetime routines over and World War II underway for the U.S., the 22nd received orders to fly to Muroc Field in California. Muri's flight log for December 1941 shows that he took off with the rest of the 22nd from Langley on the 8th. Muri, at the controls of a B-26, flew the southern route to El Paso that day, with other 22nd groups going farther north through Memphis and Albuquerque. After a stop at Barksdale Airfield in Louisiana, he reached Tucson, Arizona, on the 9th, and the next day he landed at Muroc.

Maj. Mark Lewis led the group flying the southern route. He took off from Biggs Field at Fort Bliss, the Army base at El Paso, at about 9 a.m. on Dec. 9. He had gotten airborne when one engine in his B-26, No. 40-1443, quit. With six crewmen aboard, flying at an altitude of 400 feet, Lewis tried to return to the runway, but the bomber crashed and burned three miles east of the field.

Killed in the crash beside Lewis was co-pilot Maj. Dave Laibach, the Group Executive Officer. Crew member Cpl. Francis J. Fizzier suffered severe head injuries and died soon after being hospitalized. The Army never determined the cause of the crash.

El Paso didn't make a favorable impression on Jim the first time he saw it in early December 1941. Flying from Langley Field to California, he and his crew overnighted at Biggs Field.

Decades later, Jim recalled the impression Biggs made on him and other 22nd airmen: "It was all dirt; there was no runway.

"By the time the last airplane got on the ground, there was nothing but sand all over El Paso. … [It was] nighttime – and again, I don't know whether it was good flying or luck or what, but we all did manage to get down in good shape."

The next day, December 9, he and his crew heard about the tragedy that had struck the 22nd. Jim dubbed himself "Tail-End Charlie" because he was No. 13 and last to take off within the 18th Reconnaissance Squadron (part of the 22nd). As his plane left Biggs, Jim saw the wreckage of the crash that killed the group commander and other fliers. Muri and his crewmen glanced downward, then flew on towards Muroc.

The 22nd reeled from the accident because the fliers liked and respected Lewis. However, it took a while for the news to reach the rest of the group. Maj. Dwight D. Divine, who also flew through El Paso, recorded leaving there at 8:20 a.m. on the 9th in his diary.

What awaited the members of the 22nd at the end of their cross-country flights was a 470-square-mile base atop a hard, dry lake, beneath which was a salt pan. Muroc Field, now Edwards Air Force Base, lies in Southern California's Mojave Desert near Lancaster and Rosamond.

Divine said he got to Muroc without incident, "but oh what a mess" awaited him. Muroc wasn't prepared to receive the men, and Lewis and Laibach hadn't arrived. They were dead, but Divine didn't yet know about the crash. He became the senior officer in a rugged setting.

"Finally found the east camp with stoves, floors, lights, etc. Got blankets, straw, wood, etc. Started to rain, of course. Didn't get any sleep to speak of. The lake bed is flat, hard as a rock and miles long and wide."

A town in the desert sprang up almost overnight when the Langley contingent showed up. Starting with two officers and 80 enlisted men housed in two barracks on December 7, 1941, the field's population swelled to more than 1,000 men in a few days. First tasks for the newly arrived 22nd personnel were installing water lines, digging latrines, and handling other work needed to make the base livable.

By December 10, news of the setback reached Muroc, as mentioned in Divine's diary.

"Very bad news. Mark Lewis and Dave Laibach both killed taking off from El Paso after us yesterday. (Maj. Stuart W.) McLellan (Assistant Operations Officer) seriously injured. What a blow. Both good soldiers. Mark the best I ever knew. I'm in command of the group now."

Divine soon got orders relieving him from command of the group and giving command to Maj. Millard Haskin. Jo Warner left his leadership role in the 18th, and the Army put Divine in charge of that squadron.

"Demotion or somebody using good sense, or both? Who knows? Anyway, I'm glad to be in Reconnaissance again," Divine wrote.

Muroc presented an inhospitable environment to Muri and his colleagues when they arrived in the first month of World War II. For starters, shelter from nighttime cold (and occasional rain) was less than ideal. The problem started when the 22nd's ground crews packed equipment and supplies they needed aboard boxcars at Langley for the train trip west on December 12. Mistakes in logistics meant that tents got put in one car, and tent poles, tent ropes, and tent pegs traveled in another car, the assumption being that everything would be together at journey's end.

When the men got off the train at Muroc on Dec. 15, they lacked tents, bedding, blankets and food. The railroad sidelined the train car carrying the tents en route while the car with tent parts reached the base. The Army trucked in rations from March Field but couldn't keep up with the demand. Seasonal weather also challenged the men at Muroc, who sweltered in midday heat and practically froze at night.

Men burned fires through the night to stay warm, using tent pegs for fuel, but they saved the poles for use when the tents would arrive.

"Damned cold out here tonight," Jim said to his fellow soldiers as they put on all the spare clothing they had and crowded around the fires. "Thought I left this winter weather behind in Montana." He and the other servicemen chatted and joked well into the night as a way of avoiding fitful slumber on the cold ground.

"Give me a little room," someone said as the soldiers wrapped themselves in whatever cover they could find and bedded down as close to the fire as space allowed.

Rations finally reached the 22nd Group, and tents showed up. By their third night at Muroc, most men were sleeping in canvas quarters. Air mattresses and pot-bellied wooden stoves showed up, and the fliers experienced modest comfort in time for America's first Christmas of World War II.

Jim reached Muroc on December 13, 1941. He spent December 15 on reconnaissance duty, then got orders to fly his B-26 to Tucson, where he spent five days helping patrol the Mexican border.

Reports, most false, of Japanese submarines lurking off the California coast and Japanese planes parked on Mexican soil came in. Americans, stunned by the attack on Pearl Harbor, harbored rumors of the Japanese taking the next step: attacking the U.S.

mainland. This hysteria had unfortunate consequences, notably the detention of Japanese-Americans thought to be a Fifth Column at camps in the West.

On Dec. 17, 1941, a B-26 piloted by 2nd Lt. John E. Cooper spotted something off the California coast. Cooper was part of a four-plane squadron commanded by 2nd Lt. Frank Allen ordered to report to San Diego Naval Air Station at North Island to assist the Navy in coastal patrols. The pilot swooped in on what the crew thought was an enemy submarine, but the bombardier decided the plane was too low to drop the bombs and held off.

Cooper circled back to take another look, but by then whatever he and his men had seen had vanished. If it ever existed.

At midnight on the 17th, commanders told Allen's group to get ready for another mission. The Navy had received a report of 500 Japanese planes sitting on a beach in Mexico, 400 miles south of San Diego. Group crews loaded the B-26s with bombs, and the fliers were ready to take off when word came that planes couldn't be spotted. Mission cancelled.

One incident symbolized how Muri and the rest of the 22nd had to shift from peacetime to thoughts of war. It involved a B-26 that didn't complete the initial cross-country flight because the Air Force diverted it to the Martin plant in Baltimore to have its top gun turret installed.

Private Robert A. Lauducci, a crewman on the detoured B-26, related in his diary how he and others heard about the attack on Pearl Harbor and what happened the next day, December 8.

"At morning reveille, we were told that after breakfast we were to report to the hangar and be ready to move out. Before reporting to the hangar as a bombardier, I was to report to Tech Supply for my gear, which was a flying suit, a .45-caliber automatic with holster, belt and clip of ammunition, and a new M9 bombsight.

"What brought me to reality was that I didn't have to sign for anything. Yesterday, one couldn't get a screw at Tech Supply without signing for it, and now I'm issued the Air Corps' most secret weapon as if they were giving me a can of C-rations. I was a bewildered kid growing up fast."

The M9 bombsight referenced by Lauducci was better known as the Norden Bombsight. It was a sophisticated device that used an analog computer to calculate the bomb's trajectory based on current flight conditions. Circuitry linked the bombsight to the bomber's autopilot, which let it react to changes in the wind or other effects. This resulted in unprecedented accuracy when American planes used the bombsight in daylight bombing from high altitudes.

Problems with Lauducci's B-26 turned into a quasi-comic mini saga involving the plane's bombsight. When this bomber, now equipped with a turret gun, took off from Baltimore and landed at Shreveport, Louisiana, its right engine quit. Ground crews towed the plane into a hangar to repair a cracked distributor cap that was shorting out the engine.

Distributor caps weren't available — the Army held a limited or non-existent parts inventory for the new B-26 — so Lauducci and his crew mates had to wait for a distributor cap to arrive from the Martin factory.

When mechanics found the problem and he realized he would be stuck for a few more days, Lauducci realized the predicament the precious Norden posed for him. Being responsible for it meant he would have to "babysit the bombsight and sleep in the airplane." Lauducci asked Capt. Guy Rockey what to do with the bombsight. Rockey thought for a minute and told Lauducci to wait at the plane until he, Rockey, returned.

The officer came back in a Jeep, and "he said, 'Get the bombsight and hop in the Jeep.' We took off for the Provost Marshall's office. In the PM's office Capt. Rockey confronted the (PM) captain and explained to him that the bag contained a top-secret weapon that had to be locked up and suggested (using) one of the jail cells.

"The PM replied that all cells were occupied. Capt. Rockey insisted that the bombsight must be locked up. The PM emptied a cell, and I placed a straight back chair in the middle of the room upon which I put the bombsight. The door was closed and locked, and I was free to go to town."

With the 22nd somewhat settled in at Muroc in December 1941, Jim received orders to fly B-26 patrols along the Mexican border from a Tucson base. A familiar face joined him. While in training, he had become a close friend of Lt. Merrill "Jo Jo" Dewan, a B-26 navigator, and the Army also sent Dewan to Tucson for patrol duty.

Let's get married, one of the men said. It's uncertain who instigated the idea, but Jim and Jo Jo had their fiancés, Alice Moyer and Elsie Howe, come to Arizona. The couples got married in Tucson in a double-ring ceremony on December 25, 1941.

While at March Field in early 1942, before shipping to Hawaii, Jim found time to continue something he loved and did well: playing basketball. He joined a base team coached by a fellow Montanan, James Melton, of Dillon, according to the *Dillon* (MT) *Examiner* (June 24, 1942). That connection helped Muri befriend a man then at March Field who was an early hero of the war in the Pacific. The Army belatedly awarded the Distinguished Service Cross to Master Sergeant Anthony Holub, a friend of Melton's, for bravery in helping repel Japanese air attacks on Clarke Field in the Philippines.

Holub saved the lives of the heavy-bomber crew he was part of, and the plane itself, in the December 1941 battle. He fought off Japanese pursuit planes until the American fliers could reach their airship and attack the invaders, according to the *Tucson* (AZ) *Daily Citizen* (March 2, 1942).

Holub was born in Bohemia, part of Czechoslovakia, and was not a U.S. citizen when World War II began. That prevented him from receiving the DSC for his deeds. Conferring citizenship on him so he could receive the award required a special act of Congress, according to the *Dillon Examiner* article. Melton, Muri and other servicemen in Riverside, California, took on that project.

Seven months later, the foreign-born aerial gunner got a double delight. He became an American citizen, sworn to loyalty in a Washington, D.C., district court. On the same day, he received his DSC, according to the *Cincinnati* (OH) *Enquirer* (February 25, 1943).

Army officers described Holub as a "man with ice water in his veins" and provided additional details of his heroics. Holub grabbed a machine gun inside the crowded Flying Fortress and blasted away until his ammunition ran out. He sprinted 200 yards across an open field, got more bullets from another grounded plane, ran back to his post and resumed firing. Holub, 38, served a foreign country for part of his time in uniform while his wife and their four-year-old lived in Wink, Texas.

Chapter 7 - Buildup to Battle

As 1942 began, Admiral Chester Nimitz's plan for conflict in the Pacific listed three primary Japanese intentions: attacks in the Far East leading to the capture of Malaysia, and on the Philippines and the N.E.I. (Netherlands East Indies), resulting in their capture; consolidation of this territory; and a thrust toward Australia. The planners assigned lower priority for likely Japanese offensive actions to nine fronts. At the bottom of the list was an attack to capture Midway, along with Palmyra, the main Hawaiian Islands and Oahu. Still, planners recommended covering Midway with elements of the U.S. Pacific fleet.

February 1942 found Muri and Dewan in San Francisco, awaiting the trip to Hawaii. Before the friends got to the northern California city, they spent a brief period in Alice's hometown, Riverside, an occasion that Dewan recorded in his diary.

In a February 5, 1942, entry, Dewan wrote: "Elsie and I got up about 7:30 and Susie (Alice Muri) had cooked breakfast for all of us. We had country sausage — straight from the ranch of Jim's folks in Montana ... and pancakes. It was the most wonderful night together ever. Thank God; for it was to be our last for a long, long time."

That Thursday afternoon, Merrill and Elsie Dewan went to a bank in downtown Riverside and filled out a power of attorney for her. Then the servicemen took a taxi to March Field, and at 12:30 p.m., members of the 22nd and 18th bomb groups boarded a train for San Francisco.

"It was a sad parting for all of us, but I was to see Elsie in S.F. And was glad of it. That afternoon and night were spent on a lumbering, noisy train," Dewan wrote.

Jim and other members of the 22nd took a train from Los Angeles to San Francisco in early February 1942 to begin their time of combat in the Pacific.

Jo Jo called the next day, February 6, 1942, "the most heartbreaking day in my whole life." The servicemen arrived in San Francisco and boarded the Grant at 11:30 a.m. Some of the men, including Dewan, had expected to spend a day or two with their wives before being shipped to the Pacific front, but a change in arrangements nixed those plans.

Dewan said his "sweet and dependable wife" was at the docks when he and Muri arrived to board their ship. Elsie Dewan had driven from Riverside to San Francisco with the wife of a fellow B-26 pilot and 22nd member, Herb Mayes. Alice Muri, however, said goodbye to Jim before he got on the train that took 22nd airmen from Los Angeles to San Francisco.

Dewan said he and Elsie "spent about 20 precious last minutes together and I kissed her and her held her tight and told her over and over again how much I loved her."

He closed that day's diary on a spiritual note. "I ask God to somehow right the horrible world situation as soon as possible with the least suffering to everyone. My feelings represent the feelings of thousands of our young men — of all races — who at heart do not desire to slaughter each other, but who, like myself, only ask for peace, and the right to live and love, and to let other people do the same."

At San Francisco, about 400 men from the 22nd joined Navy personnel and civilians, making about 1,400 passengers who boarded the *U.S.N.T Grant*, a Navy transport ship for the trip to Hawaii.

The *Grant* joined a convoy which included the *U.S.S. Kittyhawk*, a Navy seaplane tender that carried the 22nd's disassembled B-26s, a tanker, a Matson Navigation Company liner converted to military use, a smaller passenger ship and a freighter. Three destroyers guarded against attack by Japanese submarines.

Ships carrying the 22nd fliers, planes and equipment left San Francisco Bay on Sunday, February 8, and joined the Hawaii-bound convoy. It arrived in Honolulu a week later, on the morning of February 15. The troops ate noon dinner on their boat and then went to Hickam Field, where World War II became real to young men who not long before had left peacetime surroundings in the cities of America or, with Jim Muri, the ranch land of Montana.

"All of us were dumbstruck by the terrific amount of damage done by the Japs on December 7th. Those dirty bastards!" Dewan wrote.

"There are shell holes everywhere — and torn roofs, and machine gunned walls, and broken windows," he said, adding that he had yet to see the destruction at Pearl Harbor. At Hickam, the Corps assigned officers to wooden barracks that provided some shelter and housed enlisted men in tents.

Hickam was a prime target of the surprise Japanese attack centered on Pearl Harbor, which had drawn the U.S. into war. Japanese planes bombed and strafed the strategic airfield to keep U.S. airplanes from following the attackers back to their aircraft carriers. That tactic succeeded. It left 42 American planes destroyed and many others damaged. The human cost was high: 189 dead and 303 wounded at Hickam.

Many barely past adolescence, the 22nd airmen witnessed sobering sights at Hickam. Hulks of planes hit by bombs and bullets sat next to buildings. At one large barracks, they saw broken windows and a roof that sagged; shredded parts of outer walls looked like confetti. Inside, debris created by bombs hitting the building littered the floor between rows of bunks, their bedding gone so they offered no shelter to weary troops. Gun emplacements stood in bomb craters, defenders ready if the Japanese returned to Hawaii.

Yet, silhouetted on the horizon, a symbol of America's refusal to accept defeat flapped in the breeze. Survivors made a point of raising an enormous flag, and Old Glory flew on a pole that towered over the airfield.

Hawaii still kept its idyllic side, though, which Jim portrayed in a letter he sent to his wife soon after his arrival. After telling Alice he wasn't sure how long his unit would stay at the airfield, Muri said, "The country is all as beautiful as people say it is, and the weather is simply wonderful. It reminds me of California in the summer. I know you would like it if it were possible for you to be here."

While at Hickam, Muri got reacquainted with many airmen he had gone through flight school with. It was almost as if he were dropping in to visit a new post, similar to ones in California, that had sprung up in Hawaii.

"Very nice indeed," he said.

Other Hawaiian sights caught the Montanan's eye. "Say — you talk about 'Georgia Peaches' — 'California beauties' or 'Virginia Redheads' — you should see these Hawaiian Wahinis — now there is something for you — nope — I'm sorry Darling but I'm a married man — true to my wife — the most precious thing alive … and don't believe anything Jo Jo may have told you."

On February 16, Muri, Dewan and others in the 22nd met with an Army colonel. "He said we are to stay here and be trained for combat. Our airplanes will be assembled here and we will do many practice navigation flights," Dewan said. Then the fliers would continue to their destination and battle the Japanese.

Dewan said he and Muri spent a few minutes in a "swell" Officers' Club before going to bed.

Another meeting the next day revealed the destination for the B-26 crews. "We are going to Australia via the South Sea Islands and then to Brisbane," Jo Jo said.

On February 19, Muri and Dewan walked to the telephone exchange. Dewan scheduled a trans-Pacific call for the next evening to Elsie, his wife of less than two months. Then the two young Army friends ate supper, stopped at the club, went home and retired early.

After navigation class on the 20th, Muri and Dewan got permission from Col. Dwight Divine to take overnight leave. They headed to Honolulu, where they shopped and went to the Moana Hotel. They registered, then walked near Waikiki Beach, took pictures and dined at the hotel. Next stop was the phone exchange where Elsie's phone call came through.

"It was wonderful to hear her voice," Dewan said.

The next morning, a Saturday (February 21) brought a rude awakening for the pair. They rose at 7:30, ate breakfast at the PX and then, upon arriving back at base, learned they had spent the night "in a very high class house of prostitution (whore house!)," Dewan said.

That afternoon, Muri, Dewan and others in their bombing group flew to Bellows Field in a B-18 to stay for night for a navigation mission the next day. "This field is a dead ringer for Muroc, Calif. — dust, and sand, and all," Dewan said.

He continued his account by describing the fliers' 5 1/2-hour patrol that day. "Talk about sick! I was so sick in that damn B-18 that I thought my stomach would turn inside out." Maybe thinking of the B-26s he and Muri had flown in, Dewan said, "Give me back a smooth airplane — and one with some speed."

When Jim wrote Alice from Hawaii, poignancy and wistfulness spilled out from the pen of a soldier-turned-bomber pilot who found himself in a war several thousand miles away from the rugged Great Plains country of his youth and almost as far from the southern California home of the woman he had married two months before.

"I am lonely tonight," Jim said in a March 5, 1942, letter to Alice in Riverside.

"Although I am a million miles away from you, my heart is with you with every breath I take. Your lovely face is always before me, your smile and tender caress is my life, my love and my soul."

He shared doggerel he attributed to Dewan:

Roses are Red; Violets are Purple,

Sugar is Sweet, and so is Maple Syrple (sic)

Perhaps alluding to the lingering effects of his burst appendix and the resulting infection he suffered, Jim said he had "more help here than I really need. If this is a trifle mixed up, you'll know why."

Lt. Ed Fogarty, also stationed at Hickam, got his head shaved, but he used his shorn status to lighten up Muri and others in their immediate Army Air Force circle.

"Foggy," as they called the 22nd Group navigator, "said to tell you he is saving that last lock of hair, on his bald head, for you. Isn't that sweet of him?" Jim told Alice.

Muri reported that he purchased more slacks and shirts that day. The new attire might come in handy when the U.S. disposed of the Japanese in short order," if American hopes came true.

"Darling, I hope your rumors have some luck. They would be wonderful, especially the one where we finish this up in 18 months."

Jim said he was looking at a picture of Alice "right here in front of me and honest, honey, I feel just like reaching out and grabbing you.

"Everyone wants to know how such an ugly guy as I am rates such a beautiful wife. How do I, honey? Even I can't answer that one."

Foggy had given Muri another moniker — "Nau," which is a hard-to-read word in Jim's otherwise neat penmanship.

"Everyone [calls me] 'Nau' Muri, with an accent on the 'Nau.' We sure go around and around. Naturally, I never give in or quit.

"We have plenty of time, and it's all fun. Some of the names, though — whew! Remind me, and I'll tell you sometime."

Jim asked Alice to contact Hank Swartz's wife, Edna, living in Sacramento and pregnant with their first child. Jim wanted to find out where the Army had sent his Miles City buddy because he hoped to see him.

"Another thing. I'm writing home to get my suit. By a new order, all suits (worn by Army officers) must be single-breasted, no cuffs on the pants, small pant (unintelligible) … and short coats. Not for me, Sweetheart. I better keep the good one I have," he wrote.

Jim said he'd have his parents in Carterville send the suit he preferred to her in Riverside. That way, he'd have something pleasing to wear he came home — "and I am coming, darling."

He closed with a promise to write again the next day and a request that Alice send his love to her family. He declared he meant everything he said at the start of the letter.

Jim wrote to Alice again on March 18, 1942.

"There isn't much to write about these days, especially today, as the mail didn't come in and I did exactly nothing, sooo (sic) I shan't say much," he wrote. And then he expounded, prefacing his remarks by noting that it wasn't much after 9 p.m. in Hawaii and he couldn't go to bed yet.

He asked Alice what she had been doing. "Staying as beautiful as ever, I know, but are you as bashful? Oh, of course, you are."

Jim said his mother had saved "some swell (chicken) fryers" for Alice when she got to Montana. "Isn't that nice? Eat plenty for me, hon, cause I'll probably be eating about one meal every week by then. If I'm lucky."

Jo Jo, a New Yorker unaccustomed to tropical rays, was suffering from severe sunburn, Muri said.

"Boy, it's wonderful. Big blisters and everything. The dope. My razzing hurts worse than the actual wounds."

Jim said he was lonesome, "terribly lonesome," for his wife, an emotion he couldn't hide even from himself.

"You sure picked a lemon when it comes to happiness. I'm either gone all the time or I'm sick, or something is wrong otherwise."

He reminisced about the "great" time they had when last together in San Francisco in February 1942, before the convoy sailed to Hawaii.

"Never one word of anger in all the time we spent together; that is something that very few people can say, and to think I have made you cry.

"Ahem, I love you, Susie, love you so much that sometimes I think I am little wacky from it. If I am, I sure intend to stay that way."

Jim told Alice he symbolically kissed her each night before retiring, something he thought she might not have known.

"I hope I don't disturb your sleep doing it. It's nothing new … I've been doing it since December 28, 1940. Some time ago, isn't it?

Muri said that while he conversed with another officer, he showed the man pictures Alice had sent. That individual, a lieutenant, said, "Damned if that isn't Hank," and Jim decided the hunch he and Alice had was right. Swartz was somewhere in the sprawling military complex on Oahu, and Jim vowed to look up his fellow Montanan soon.

Muri turned to a topic he said his wife wouldn't like: his mortality as a soldier at war.

He said he was writing her now because with censorship and interruptions in mail delivery, he might not get a reply from Alice for months.

"It's something I've been thinking about for some time now and couldn't talk about to you. Don't get me wrong, dear, as it is about what I would want you to do if anything happened to me."

He said mail might go through only every three months, maybe every six months, maybe not all.

"I don't want you to worry if you don't hear anything, though.

Darn, hon, I sure am a pessimist, aren't I? I always get that way when I don't have anything to write about."

Jim mentioned his sister-in-law, Margaret Moyer, and her boyfriend and wondered when they planned to marry. Soon, he hoped, passing on his regards.

Jim said he had forgotten earlier and now wanted to tell Alice about getting their car and driving it. She'd need a driver's license and a sticker for the windshield, something her brother, Charles, could help with.

He closed by saying he planned to go to bed early.

"I love you oodles and oodles, dearest. Keep pitching, and I'll try and hurry home," he said.

In the vast Pacific expanse, another young serviceman from West Virginia was beginning his tour of duty with the Navy. He would hear about Jim, but six decades would pass before their paths crossed. Two other Montanans, also in the Army Air Force, were preparing to help write history for their part in a legendary bombing mission.

Chapter 8 – Pacific Preliminaries

Jim's duties at Hickam Field remained the same in March and April 1942: reassembling B-26s taken apart on the West Coast and shipped to Hawaii. Meanwhile, two fellow Montanans, both members of the Army Air Corps, continued preparations for their roles in a Pacific theater mission. They were among 80 men who took part in Jimmy Doolittle's mid-April 1942 raid, a bold achievement that would gain lasting fame and seal the Japanese military's determination to strike Midway. As Muri and the Treasure State Doolittle Raiders continued their duties, a teenager from West Virginia who had signed up for the Navy at age 16 arrived in Hawaii.

That youngster, Lonnie Bell, would take part in the Battle of Coral Sea, the early May 1942 engagement that served as a dress rehearsal for Midway. Two decades later, he ended up in Billings, Montana, and continued his career as a country music radio broadcaster and musician. While in Billings, he wrote a song to honor veterans of Vietnam, World War II and the Korean conflict. The song, first aired in 1976, includes lines about an Army pilot Bell didn't know then — Muri — who skimmed the full length of a Japanese carrier deck and then evaded enemy fire to return to his base. It would take another 25 years before Lonnie and Jim would meet in Billings, which Jim called home for the final dozen years of his life.

Combat in the Pacific expanded in the spring of 1942, and Bell experienced historic events that shaped his life. After the war ended, the native of Enterprise, West Virginia worked as a country music disc jockey on radio stations in Honolulu and made that his career after he left the Navy and moved back to the mainland in 1959. Bell worked at stations in Washington state and Oregon before landing a job in Billings in 1964. He worked in Montana's largest city for 54 years, became a country music broadcasting legend and retired in 2018 just before he turned 94.

Bell grew up in coal-mining country but decided he wanted to do something else with his life. He signed up for the Navy in November 1940, went through boot camp and was stationed in Newfoundland when a thunderbolt hit. "Everyone knows what happened on December 7, 1941," he recalled decades later.

Pearl Harbor shaped his life in a way he couldn't have imagined, as it did with millions of other young Americans. The next day, December 8, Bell and fellow Navy aviators flew to the South Pacific. The last 600-mile leg of a journey halfway around the world put them 800 miles off the coast of Australia at New Caledonia, where they flew patrol duty to search for an expected Japanese thrust. Bell took part in air patrols near Guadalcanal, which Japan invaded in the summer of 1942. Navy and Marine defenders held off the invasion in the most savage battle in the Pacific; the Americans prevailed near year's end.

Two other native Montanans prepared in the spring of 1942 for a mission as storied as the Battle of Midway. They were Edward Saylor and David Thatcher, two of the 80 Doolittle Raiders. Saylor, a fellow product of a ranch background, hailed from Garfield County, a sparsely populated district that bordered Rosebud County, the place of Jim Muri's birth in Eastern Montana. Thatcher grew up in Bridger, Montana, a town south of Billings.

Final training for Doolittle's plucky group, members of the 17th

Bomb Group (Medium), occurred where Jim Muri was stationed for two years starting in October 1942. That was Eglin Field in the Florida panhandle where the chosen pilots and crews practiced taking off on a short stretch of runway. A Navy officer guided them through simulations of takeoff from an aircraft carrier, but neither he nor Army officers on hand told the men anything about their mission until after cranes lifted their planes aboard the *USS Hornet* in San Francisco Bay and the ship sailed west into the Pacific.

A string of battle reverses made the first half of 1942 a dark time for soldiers, sailors and airmen, and the American public back home. Then came electrifying news. Doolittle piloted a B-25 bomber that took from the *Hornet*, the lead plane of 16 Mitchells that flew 600 miles and struck Japan on a daylight bombing run over Tokyo and nearby cities.

Bell and his comrades, stationed at New Caledonia, heard about the raid soon after it happened.

"The Doolittle Raid had a lot of effect on morale," which was very low, he said.

"Those early days of the war saw the USA losing, it seemed, at every location on the map. We had lost at Pearl Harbor, Wake Island and the Philippines. It seemed that all news was bad news."

The Doolittle Raid, followed by three major battles in the Pacific later that year, all U.S. victories, would lift American spirits. Like a boxer decked by his opponent's wicked punch who rises and knocks out his nemesis, the U.S. rallied from the Pearl Harbor and Philippines debacles and out-punched Japan in a long, costly match.

Chance put the two Montanans who took part in the Doolittle

Raid within walking distance of each other at the start of an ordeal after they reached China. Thatcher was the navigator on a B-25 nicknamed *Ruptured Duck*, which became the most famous plane involved in the raid. Ted Lawson piloted *Ruptured Duck*, which crashed hard off the coast of China and ended up just a few miles from where Saylor's plane crashed. Thatcher, Saylor and other Raiders avoided capture by Japanese troops, traveled across China and through the Middle East to Africa, and then caught flights to Brazil. They reached the U.S. in late summer 1942, concluding a zigzag route home caused by Nazi Germany's control of much of Europe.

Thanks to Lawson, the raid gained silver screen fame while World War II still raged. Lawson wrote a best-selling account of the raid, "Thirty Seconds Over Tokyo," which Hollywood adapted as a movie of the same name.

The Doolittle Raid caused little damage to Japanese military facilities bombed in and near Tokyo. Yet its psychological impact was profound. Having 16 American warplanes attack the heart of the nation's defense, within striking distance of the emperor's place, obliterated the long-held Japanese belief that their island nation was unconquerable. The raid was a thunderclap equivalent to the one Americans heard when Japan struck Pearl Harbor.

Six days before the raid, the plan to strike Midway reached the desk of the general who headed operations for the Japanese Army's general staff. The Army challenged the push to attack Midway, which it viewed as a step toward the Navy's larger goal, the capture of Hawaii, which would extend Japan's defense perimeter in the Pacific to the breaking point. The Navy flexed its muscles, overruled the Army and sent a proposal for the Midway operation to Emperor Hirohito on April 16.

While the military awaited a decision, the American B-25s showed up. "It was if a shiver had passed over Japan," said Kameto Kuroshima, a high-level ranking member of the Japanese Navy.

Historian Samuel Eliot Morison said the Japanese Navy's plan to grab Midway and the far reaches of the Aleutian Islands sped up in the spring of 1942. "Capture of these islands was the most important objective in the second great Japanese offensive that began with the drive on Port Moresby, to end with the conquest of Samoa, Fiji and Noumea," he said, and conquest of the American outposts gained added importance to shore up Japan's "ribbons defense," which Doolittle's raid had pierced.

Admiral Yamamoto, commander of the Combined Fleet, took a strategic view. He had studied in the U.S. during the 1920s and understood America's industrial might and vast supplies of materials and skilled workers. Knowing those resources would favor the U.S. in a war of attrition, Yamamoto argued that his country's best course was a quick strike against a high-value American possession to draw out Nimitz's Pacific Fleet. Once the American carriers sailed beyond their West Coast and Pearl Harbor bases, the Japanese Navy could launch waves of planes to sink the carriers and conquer Nimitz's fleet once and for all. Everything pointed to a pounce on Midway.

Yamamoto's influence resulted in a May 5, 1942, order from Imperial Headquarters: "Commander in Chief, Combined Fleet, will, in cooperation with the Army, invade and occupy strategic points in the Western Aleutians and Midway Island."

Yamamoto issued orders for the Midway operation on May 12, followed by orders on May 18 for capture of New Caledonia, Fiji and Samoa. Seizure of the latter trio of islands was the second phase of Japan's plan to ensure a defensive barrier against the U.S. in the Pacific.

"The Japanese at this time evidently considered that their operations in the Coral Sea had been advantageous, even though they had not succeeded in capturing Port Moresby," according to the U.S. Navy's 1948 Midway Strategic and Tactical Analysis publication. The Japanese believed they sank the *Saratoga* and *Yorktown* on May 8; neither U.S. carrier had gone down, although *Yorktown* had returned to Pearl Harbor for repairs of damage it had sustained in the battle. The Japanese also thought they had drawn two additional U.S. carriers into the Coral Sea area on May 14.

Information collected by the U.S. after Japan's surrender in August 1945 showed that the Doolittle Raid ratcheted up pressure to implement the plan for further strikes in the South Pacific and against Midway. A Japanese combat account, *The Battle of the Coral Sea*, said the plucky B-25 crews who bombed Tokyo and other hubs of Japanese war industry constituted a "cheering" mission that really was "only a nuisance raid."

Admiral Ernest King, commander-in-chief of the U.S. Fleet, however, gave the Doolittle Raid more importance. "Whatever the damage inflicted by these bombers, the attack was stimulating to morale, which at that time, considering the surrender of Bataan and the situation in general in the Far East, was at low ebb," he said.

Nimitz, taking advantage of intelligence findings from Navy codebreakers that pointed to Japanese designs on Midway, planned the defense of the atoll throughout May 1942 with full belief it would require a coordinated effort involving the Navy, Marines and the Army. On May 23, he directed his staff to discuss the issue with Major General Clarence Tinker, head of the Army's 7th Air Force. Planners told military chiefs in Hawaii to supply "maximum of effect from the Army and Navy air strength in the Hawaiian Islands in defeating Japanese attacks on Midway and/or any of the main islands of the Hawaiian Group — without exposing our carriers to danger of destruction out of proportion to the damage they can inflict."

Planners would have to calculate the risk and accept associated danger if outweighed by the odds of stopping the Japanese strike or sinking enemy carriers. "Our air force — both Army and Navy — must be employed with maximum skill and such attacks as we attempt must be carried out with the greatest determination."

Nimitz formalized the U.S. arrangement for the Battle of Midway on May 27 in CINPAC's Op-Plan 29-42. It called for three task forces organized around carriers: TF16, commanded by Rear Admiral Raymond Spruance, with *Enterprise* and *Hornet*; TF 17, commanded by Rear Admiral Jack Fletcher, with *Yorktown*; and TF11, commanded by Rear Admiral Audrey Fitch, with *Saratoga*. *Saratoga*, however, was being repaired on the West Coast and was unavailable. The Navy organized Pearl Harbor-based submarines in TF7, commanded by Rear Admiral Robert English.

The plan called on Marines stationed on Midway to hold the base. Also, the Army received a specific role — the Hawaiian Department was to contribute "long-range bomber and torpedo carrying aircraft" that would conduct missions assigned by the commander of Midway's Naval Air Station, Cyril Simard.

B-26s continued to arrive in Hawaii in late May 1942 as preparations continued for defense against the almost certain

Japanese attack on Midway, the atoll at the northwest end of the island chain. The Air Corps scheduled twenty-six Marauders to show up at Hickam on May 19. It would take about one day after arrival for crews to replace ordnance and other material removed when airmen flew the planes in from the mainland; that extra equipment went by other air transportation.

The B-26s that arrived that spring had torpedo racks, but their pilots and crews still needed torpedo training.

On May 22, the Commander of the Navy's Hawaiian Department updated the Navy chief of staff about training the B-26 fliers in use of the unfamiliar weapon. Time was running out — it was less than two weeks before the battle — but the Navy had prepared tactical and technical training for B-26 crews who would fight at Midway and elsewhere in the Pacific.

"COMINCH [King] wants the Army to learn to drop torpedoes from B-26s," the *Graybook* noted on May 2. Then came what may not have been a sardonic comment.

"The Navy has something to learn on that." That is, dropping torpedoes.

On May 31, the Hawaiian department commander reported to Washington that four B-26s were in combat readiness at Midway, along with 15 B-17s. More Flying Fortresses were on the way.

Earlier in May 1942, Lonnie Bell and his fellow Catalina airmen at New Caledonia knew nothing of the Japanese intra-service machinations and little of what was being discussed by their commanders in Honolulu and on Midway. All they could tell was that big things were about to happen in waters close to them, off the coast of Australia.

"We flew over the (U.S.) aircraft carrier *Lexington* just sitting out in water. Someone said they are waiting for the fleet, and sure enough they were. They were in a big battle called the Battle of the Coral Sea," Bell said in 2017.

The Coral Sea clash ended with mixed results, although the U.S. won a strategic victory. *Lexington* went to the bottom, sunk by a torpedo from an Allied destroyer to avoid having the enemy capture the carrier after hits from two torpedoes and two bombs fatally damaged her. The other U.S. carrier in the battle, the *Yorktown*, suffered a bomb hit that killed 66 men, but the Navy got her back to Pearl Harbor and crews performed near-miraculous repairs in three days, work that ordinarily would have required weeks or months to accomplish.

The Americans won the Coral Sea battle because of their own mistake, the happenstance sighting and sinking of the light Japanese carrier *Shoho*. A search plane from the Yorktown reported it had sighted two heavy cruisers and two destroyers 175 miles away, but that became a mistaken message related to Admiral Jack Fletcher on the Yorktown that the plane had spotted two carriers and four heavy cruisers. The Navy didn't discover the mix-up until *Yorktown* and *Lexington* dive-bombers were in the air. They continued flying and found the *Shoho*, sinking it in just 10 minutes.

Losing *Shoho* made Admiral Shigeyoshi Inouye retreat. As important, bombs launched from American planes smashed into another Japanese carrier, *Shōkaku*, and bent her flight deck so that the ship could no longer launch planes. She had to return to dry dock for repairs. *Shōkaku* had taken part in the Pearl Harbor attack. So did another carrier, *Zuikaku*, which lost so many planes in the Coral Sea she was out of service for a month getting replacement aircraft.

"Thus, neither big (Japanese) flattop could take part in the great battle coming up. But Yorktown could and did."

At Midway, the countdown to battle continued.

"Hey, watch this," a Marine enlisted man said to a group of servicemen watching his antics at Midway. "This is the gooney bird dance."

Showing, he bent his arms at the elbows and drew them close to his chest, then strutted in the sand at Eastern Island, one of the two main islands in the Midway atoll. He tried to mimic the motions of the albatrosses, called gooney birds, that servicemen saw everywhere on the spit of land at the north end of the Hawaiian Island chain.

The Marine didn't mind the good-natured heckling his audience tossed at him.

"I'm going to bring this dance with me when I go back to the states; it's gonna be the rage," he said. The servicemen clapped and cheered, happy for a break in the tension and boredom they were experiencing in the late spring of 1942.

Among those on Midway waiting for orders at the start of June 1942 were the crew of *Susie-Q*, which besides Montanan Muri included a pair of Southern Californians, Lieutenant Pren L. Moore and Lieutenant Russell Johnson.

Recalling the appearance and personalities of his crew 40-plus years after the battle, Muri described the brown-eyed, 5-foot-10 Moore as having a medium build with black hair. He laughed easily and was a storyteller. Moore, an excellent photographer who developed his own pictures, made a living with his camera on the staff of a newspaper in El Centro, California, before enlisting. His fine voice got him vocal roles in community theater productions.

Johnson was quiet and somewhat withdrawn, according to Muri. He was a loner and although a competent officer and bombardier, the other crewmen never really knew what he was thinking.

Pennsylvanian John Gogoj, a staff sergeant who was a gunner on the mission, was "always happy and smiling even when he shouldn't be," Muri said. The 5-foot-8 Gogoj sported a "wild shock of black hair" to complement his brown eyes. His dependability meant that "when he said something, that's the way it was." Gogoj, a team player who helped others, was known for his excellent knowledge of the plane and its workings.

Corporal Frank Melo, another slender airman with black hair and brown eyes, hailed from Long Island. Muri remembered him as a good radio man, an excellent gunner and someone always on the job and willing to pitch in.

The rest of the crew had to adjust to the manner of Private Earl Ashley. His upbringing in Williamston, South Carolina, resulted in Ashley having a Southern accent "so thick you couldn't believe it. Took forever to tell you something, but was smiling all the time," Muri said.

Ashley became a photographer, and when he left the AAF and returned to civilian life, he owned and operated a camera shop. His battle wounds required a lengthy hospital stay in Hawaii before the Army brought him stateside for further care. The rest of the crew moved on to other deployments and lost track of Ashley until 1985, when they located him living in retirement in Orlando, Florida.

Ill-informed or uninformed, Jim and his crew didn't have to wait long for the mission that would define their lives.

Chapter 9 - "What Kind of a Target?"

"Anybody got the dope on what's up?" a member of the *Susie-Q* crew said as Jim and other Army airmen stood around at Midway.

"Enough of the gooney birds."

They had grown tired of watching albatross antics after three or four days spent waiting for word on their mission.

June 4, 1942, started the same as five previous mornings since May 30, the first full day the airmen spent on Midway. Muri and his crew again bedded down close to *Susie-Q* — the nickname Muri's plane shared with his wife of five months, fretting about his welfare in Southern California. By 3:15 a.m., they had started the plane's engines. The powerful twin Pratt & Whitney motors snorted at startup, sounding similar to a large farm tractor or perhaps a Model T.

Jim watched his instrument panel. The oil temperature gauge showed 40 degrees, and the cylinder head pressure gauge hovered between 100 and 200 degrees. "Everything is on the beam," he said to Pren Moore. *Susie-Q*'s engines settled into a smooth throb. Crew members looked them over and found nothing amiss, so as they had done on earlier days, they shut the plane down and went on standby. They had nothing to do until dawn, at about 6 a.m., when they restarted the engines. Assured that the plane's mechanisms were flight-ready, the men shut the bomber down again.

On previous days at Midway, Muri and his crew had had little to do other than wait. Besides gooney-bird watching, the men endured pushy Marine Raiders trying to get cuts in the lines where everyone stood to get packs of cigarettes and meals dished out on tin plates at the mess hall. Card games and letter-writing filled much of their spare time.

Something seemed different when *Susie-Q*'s crew woke and started the bomber on June 4. The Marauder men, as B-26 fliers were called, had chatted with Marines manning Midway's ground defense and Navy pilots and their crews sent to the atoll. That day, the air crackled with a sense that action on the atoll and above the ocean was imminent. The men heard Navy Catalina planes, scouting for Japanese warships, take off from Eastern Island. They also heard the rumble of Army B-17s, heavy bombers heading toward the Pacific; the *Susie-Q* crew didn't know it then, but the Flying Fortresses were trying to find enemy ships approaching Midway and bomb them from high altitude.

Anticipation was almost over.

It might have been tempting for someone to light a cigarette. Many servicemen, including several of *Susie-Q*'s crew members, were smokers, the norm for American men. The military obliged by suppling servicemen with packs of Camels, Chesterfields and Lucky Strikes, popular brands of the time.

Nighttime blackout restrictions included a ban on cigarette smoking. Even the flame of a match or the glow of a cigarette tip might tip Japanese submarines patrolling off Midway to a formidable American force on the atoll. If someone lit up, "Put it out!" would have rang out.

Besides *Susie-Q*, three other B-26s, parked in concrete revetments on Eastern Island, were on standby. Twenty-eight young men, seven per plane, huddled around four bombers.

Overhead, the Herdsman and Scorpius constellations splashed the southern sky. Someone with binoculars might have picked out individual stars within the clusters. Jupiter was visible, and those with keen vision might have spotted Mars and Saturn. To the north, a cold front, with showers and clouds, limited the airmen's view.

Still, it was difficult to see their surroundings, so Muri and his fellow airmen walked carefully around a small but well-defended base. Marines assigned primary responsibility for Midway's ground defense had set up pill boxes and installed explosives that someone could detonate with a gunshot. Defenders had rolled out barbed wire. Eastern Island and adjoining Sandy Island were a thicket of preparation for an enemy attack.

Muri checked off the names of his six crew members. All present standing close to *Susie-Q*, which remained parked near the runway; all wondering if they would see combat.

Muri and Moore, peacetime enlistees, were part of America's armed forces that would swell to millions of men and women during wartime.

While President Franklin Roosevelt and Allied leaders, especially British Prime Minister Winston Churchill, tried to forge a Germany-first strategy for the war, many Americans implored the country to avenge Japan's attack on Pearl Harbor. Muri and the rest of the small group of B-26 airmen at Midway shared the sentiment, but higher-ranking officers told the Marauder Men nothing about how they and their planes might help achieve the goal of halting Japan's rampage across the Pacific.

Meanwhile, the warm waters of the Pacific Ocean northwest of Midway contained mortal danger, a threat to the survival of Muri

101

and his compatriots. Closing to within 200 miles from the U.S. base early on June 4, the Imperial Japanese Navy's Combined Fleet was ready to attack, but that was a secret kept from Army and Marine pilots defending Midway, and Marine troops manning guns near the shores. The Navy pilots on land that morning may have learned a few details of what lay ahead.

Yamamoto's fleet slipped out of the anchorage at Hashirajima in Japan's Inland Sea on May 27, 1942 and completed its departure two days later. The embarkation date carried powerful symbolism; it was Navy Day in Japan, when the nation commemorated the anniversary of Admiral Togo's 1907 victory over the Russians at Tsushima, which brought Japan into the Great Power ranks. Headed toward Midway in late May 1942 were about 190 ships, including 11 battleships, eight aircraft carriers, 23 cruisers, 65 destroyers and dozens of support vessels, a massive flotilla spread 1,800 miles across the Pacific from the Kuriles to Guam.

Japan's strike force included the carriers of Kido Butai, the force commanded by Admiral Chuichi Nagumo, which represented the Combined Fleet's most powerful weapon. Japan planned a twin-pronged attack against Midway that called for using four carriers and about 260 planes in that phase, with a smaller force to strike and occupy islands at the far western end of the Aleutian Island chain of Alaska. Altogether, about 700 sea- and land-based warplanes were at the disposal of Admiral Yamamoto, overall commander of the Combined Fleet. His command included twenty admirals and the attack force pyramid broadened to 100,000 troops, many of them part of a planned occupation force.

Two objectives guided the Combined Fleet as it sailed toward a showdown with the U.S.: to invade and seize Midway for use as a forward base in Japan's relentless march across the Pacific and Indian oceans; and to draw out and ambush U.S. carriers that had escaped the destruction at Pearl Harbor because they were at sea that day.

Ideally, from Japan's standpoint, the Combined Fleet would land a roundhouse blow that would cause the U.S. to sue for peace. Japanese military leaders with a knowledge of U.S. industrial capabilities, notably Yamamoto, feared that if their country attacked, it would rouse the so-called sleeping giant. If the U.S. could rev up its factories and induct millions of men into the military, that would cause a war of attrition that resource-poor Japan was certain to lose.

Unknown to the Japanese, Navy Lieutenant Commander Joseph Rochefort, head of the communications intelligence unit at Pearl Harbor (Station "Hypo"), and his staff had cracked the IJN code. Rochefort took his findings to Navy Lieutenant Commander Edwin Layton, the Nimitz intelligence officer, and Layton brought them to his boss. Nimitz and his inner circle expected a Japanese attack against Midway in early June. Now, with the *Yorktown*, the *Enterprise* and the *Hornet* positioned off Midway, the U.S. was ready to spring a trap of its own.

Back on Eastern Island, Muri was unaware of Hypo's intelligence findings. Two other B-26 pilots – Herb Mayes and William Watson – also knew nothing definite about the threat, although squadron leader Jim Collins may have been briefed. It's unclear whether another unit sitting on Eastern Island and awaiting orders to take off — pilots and crews of six Navy Avenger planes, part of VT-8, the torpedo squadron aboard *Enterprise* — had been briefed about the Japanese arrow pointed at Midway. The

Avengers had arrived at Honolulu too late to travel with their carrier, so the Navy ordered them to fly to Midway, thus strengthening what U.S. military planners called an unsinkable aircraft carrier.

Rather than dwell on strategic issues discussed by presidents, prime ministers, generals, and admirals, Jim focused on basics. Duty called, and he answered.

"I got in just as I turned 18," he recalled about his enlistment decades later, "but it was part of what we were supposed to do. Somebody said, 'This you must do,' (and) we did it. We attempted to do it. So that was that, we went out and did it."

He thought often of his young wife living with her mother in Southern California. Letters from Alice updated him on her family and other Army wives and sometimes they brought news of Muri's family back in Eastern Montana. He also wondered where in the Pacific a fellow Miles City pilot in the Army Air Force, Hank Swartz, was flying at that moment.

Lieutenant Mayes, one of the B-26 pilots and one of Muri's friends since they joined the 22nd Bomb Group, went into the operations building to scan the latest reports on weather and enemy sightings. A foggy day greeted the Marauder men, with clouds at 2,000 feet. Muri, his men, and the rest of the B-26 fliers climbed into their planes and restarted the engines.

Just then, Army liaison officer Jo Warner rolled up to the revetments, stopped his Jeep and jumped out. He briefed Collins: Fly a course of 320 degrees to the northwest, go 180 miles, look for a "target" and attack. Hearing those orders, Muri might have thought them as murky as the fog bank the B-26s flew through from Hickam to Midway.

"What kind of a target?" a puzzled Muri said.

"We always laughed and said, well, we'll probably get an old freighter or something out there that we can practice on. We didn't realize that there's 150 ships out there that was the target," Jim said, recalling the moments before takeoff in a video that the World War II museum created decades later.

"They gave us a heading and distance and away we went, not knowing if it was a merchant ship or carrier, or what it was," he said.

"We'd never been in combat. We didn't have any idea."

Commanders ordered the Navy's Avenger torpedo bombers and PBY Catalinas to take off first. "You guys are faster," higher-ranking officers told the Marauder pilots and crews, the assumption being they would catch up with the other planes. But if it appeared to the Japanese they were being hit by a coordinated attack, that was a false impression. No plan existed to have the Army and Navy torpedo bombers attack in concert.

"Don't use your radios," Mayes said before he took off, right behind Captain Collins, commander of the four-plane unit. By 6:15 a.m., the B-26s were airborne. Unknown to the Americans, four Japanese carriers, the core of a powerful fleet, were nearing Midway and had already launched planes to attack U.S ground defenses on the atoll. The first inkling Jim got that this would not be a ho-hum mission was when he and other pilots, flying northwest, saw waves of Japanese Zeros and dive bombers coming in to attack Midway.

None of us has ever fired a shot or taken one in battle, Jim mused as he reached for a Camel cigarette, one of 100 smokes in a can he had stashed between the seats with the lid off. He put a cigarette in his mouth and hunted for a match. He couldn't find one, so lighting it would have to wait until a less-frenzied moment.

Jim glanced at the instrument panel and concentrated on flying his "hot rod," the label the B-26 had gained since being rushed straight from production into use by Army units, with no testing, starting in 1940. The term came from the plane's speed, which topped out at 350 mph and gave it the ability to keep up with or outrun fighter planes. The B-26's short wings and high wing loading required pilots to carry out immediate responses when flying low, slow and heavy — a common occurrence during landing and takeoff. Make a mistake in those situations, and the B-26 would crash, often with fatal results. That unfortunate track record had given the plane its "widow maker" nickname, something that skilled pilots (including Jimmy Doolittle) tried to refute with demonstration flights designed to show the plane's reliability — and the need for well-trained pilots.

Susie-Q and the other B-26s carried 2,000-pound Navy M13 torpedoes in racks underneath the keel of the planes. American torpedoes proved inferior to those used by the Japanese and were almost useless in combat in the early years of the war. To make matters worse, Jim and the other Army pilots received hurried, superficial torpedo training from Navy torpedo specialists before the B-26s left Hickam Field. Jim, though, had no time to ponder the capabilities of his new weapon or its effective use. Finding the target — Japanese shipping in the vast reaches of the Pacific — was his priority. It was useless to dwell on the deficiencies of the torpedo or the quality of training he had received.

Is this the best way to fight a war? Jim asked himself. He didn't know what Admiral Nimitz was thinking, that he had decided he needed more torpedo-equipped planes on Midway ready to attack Japanese ships. The B-26s, which shipped from the Glenn Martin Co. factory in Baltimore with the capability of carrying either torpedoes or land bombs, seemed ideal to bolster Navy firepower on the atoll and in planes aboard carriers patrolling the central Pacific. Thus, Jim and the other B-26 airmen found themselves de facto Navy fliers that day.

A few minutes after *Susie-Q* took off, bombardier Russell Johnson slipped into the cramped nose where he would operate a .50-caliber machine gun. The gunners — Melo, Ashley, and Gogoj — moved into turret and tail positions.

Susie-Q was ready for battle. The rumor mill at Midway may have tipped off some of Muri's crewmen, prompting them to talk about targets the night before they took off. If a Japanese carrier showed up, they agreed to try bagging it.

Susie-Q's men polished her before they left Hickam, hoping for extra speed, which may have helped Jim to catch and pass Mayes' plane. Crews in the two B-26s exchanged waves.

Susie-Q barreled through the early-morning sky. Jim looked out the window to his right and saw sparkling lights. They almost looked like a Christmas tree. Then the realization hit him. "Hell, they're shooting at us."

It took about 40 minutes for Collins' fast four-plane group to reach a target larger than any flier could have imagined, a firepower-packed group of warships that made up Japan's Kido Butai.

"Meatballs" ahead, the Americans said over their plane intercoms. That term, used by U.S. servicemen, referred to the distinctive insignia on Japanese planes and ships, which featured the sun at the center of the Japanese "Land of the Rising Sun" flag. Muri's crew heard him over the intercom: "Get ready; the fleet is up ahead." Arrayed across the horizon were dozens of ships, four carriers at the center of a protective ring of battleships, carriers, and destroyers.

It was about 7:10 a.m. Since he hadn't found a match, Jim chomped on his unlit Camel. Then he saw smoke on the horizon ... and destroyers ... and about 50 Zeroes, the feared Japanese fighter planes. The B-26s drew closer to their assigned target. They were 50 to 100 feet off the water when "a whole flock of Japanese ships" appeared on the horizon, Jim said decades later, recalling the battle. "They were everywhere," with destroyers sailing in front of the main fleet.

Zeroes swarmed toward the four B-26s, bunched in a diamond formation when they took off. That broke up under enemy fire.

"The hell with that. We're going in," Jim said over the intercom.

The Zeroes seemed to come out of nowhere, and their pilots drew a bead on the B-26s, bent on destruction of the American planes before they could hit the Japanese fleet.

Collins, flying at the spear of the B-26s' diamond formation, saw the onrushing Zeroes, then spotted the prize of the armada — four Japanese carriers, each capable of launching dozens of planes. They sailed at the center of the massive flotilla, too well-protected for an attack on the near side. Follow me, the Mississippian signaled, and he led his pilots, with Jim in the rear slot, to starboard.

The Americans had no time or room to fly above the destroyers protecting the carriers. To launch their torpedoes and have them run true toward a ship, the B-26 pilots needed to hug the water.

They flew just a few hundred feet above the ocean. When defenders blocked the way, the B-26s had to bank upward and hurdle the obstacles.

The Americans also had to avoid getting shot down by anti-aircraft fire booming from every ship in the area, or by the fusillade of machine gun bullets and cannon shells blasting from the Zeroes. As a further challenge, Jim and the other pilots had to look out for columns of water towering in front of the B-26s. Japanese defenders pointed the big guns toward the ocean ahead of the bombers, trying to land shells that would send up pillars of water, similar to a concrete wall, that would destroy a plane on impact.

It was a madhouse, a riot of sound, sights, and fright that swelled over 28 Americans in the B-26s. So, this is war, Jim thought. He tried to stay focused on his task — launching his torpedo into the hull of a ship — but his lips trembled and the tendons stuck out in his neck. His shoulders drew tight. Fear filled the plane.

A huge flattop drew Jim's attention. He didn't know which ship it was — it turned out to be *Akagi* — but that carrier became the target no one mentioned back at Midway.

Chapter 10 - "Just as Thick as Fleas"

At about the same time Jim and his crew spotted *Akagi*, six Navy Avengers began their attack. The torpedo planes had taken off from Midway ahead of the B-26s, but the Army bombers' superior speed allowed them to arrive almost as a group with their Navy counterparts.

That led the Japanese observers to think they were undergoing a coordinated "anvil" attack by 10 torpedo planes swarming toward the carriers. This would involve using a knot of planes that would coordinate their strike against a ship by dropping torpedoes from three different head-on bearings. That would leave the ship's captain no out; no matter which way he turned, his ship would present a broadside target to at least one torpedo.

But if the Japanese thought the B-26 pilots were part of an attack that sophisticated, they were mistaken. The Marauder men received Torpedo Training 101 at Hickam — they learned a few fundamentals but nothing as advanced as anvil attack methods.

Gunners on *Susie-Q* and the other B-26s kept blazing as the formation got closer to Kido Butai. Then the Zeroes picked up the bombers, and that's when problems started.

Japanese fighters strafed *Susie-Q* from both sides and above, creating a racket that reminded Jim of what he heard growing up on an Eastern Montana ranch.

"It sounded like hail hitting a tin roof," he recalled years later.

About then, *Susie-Q's* intercom crackled, and Jim heard an excited American voice shout over the radio.

"If my momma could see me now. Ya hoo!"

Collins and Muri spotted *Akagi*, but to the carrier's right "there were six Zeroes wing to wing so we had turn left to keep from hitting the Zeros head on," Collins said after the battle.

He and Jim maneuvered to give themselves room to make a 180-degree turn and line up for another shot at the big ship. "Which worked out very good," Collins said, except that the B-26 formation wasn't tight, which allowed the Zeroes to overtake Mayes and Watson.

"Muri and I were up forward, and we weren't bothered as much with the fighters as the other two planes were," Collins recalled. He never knew whether Zeroes shot down the B-26s flown by Mayes and Watson or whether ship anti-aircraft fire splashed them. By whatever means, all 14 men aboard those bombers died that day.

Susie-Q closed in on *Akagi*. Pren Moore swung the torpedo sight into launch position, and Jim dropped the plane lower, trying not to pick up excess speed going into his torpedo run. Off to one side, he caught sight of Navy torpedo planes and Marine dive bombers downed by Japanese fighters and anti-aircraft guns in futile attempts to attack the fleet. They shot down all but one of the Navy Avengers.

"I got the nose down and held the plane on the water ... [The] fighters ... were in there just as thick as fleas. That was the first I'd heard bullets hitting an airplane, and they were hitting my airplane," Jim said decades after the battle.

"We were ducking and dodging, and ducking and skiddin' and slippin' and slidin' and everything you could think of to keep away from the Zeroes. And I'm 400, 500 feet off the water, so I got lined up on a good 45-degree angle on the target,"

With *Susie-Q's* nose down, Jim leveled the craft above the water, getting ready to launch the torpedo. Everywhere he looked, he saw speedy Japanese fighter planes, lightly armored but agile, piloted by skilled airmen who had gained a reputation for slicing up slower, less maneuverable American and Allied aircraft in the early months of the war.

"Launch the torpedo!" Jim shouted to Pren Moore. Moore leveled the torpedo sight. He was on the mark. He squeezed the trigger and twisted the plug. Again. And again, to make sure. An improvised switch, comprising a trigger, a cable and a plug with prongs seemed to have foiled the co-pilot's effort to release the 2,000-pound fish, but nobody in *Susie-Q's* cabin was sure what had happened.

As Jim looked through the windshield toward the ocean, he tried to see the wake from *Susie-Q's* torpedo, if it had launched. Looking toward Moore, Muri hollered, "Is it away?" He tried to speak above the roar of *Susie-Q's* engines, the decibels amplified by the pounding the Marauder was taking from a swam of Zero fighter planes. The anti-aircraft fire from Japanese ships added to the din.

"How the hell do I know?" Moore yelled back.

Moore and the others had experienced the sensation of a bomber rising in flight after it dropped its bomb load, but this was different. Not only was this the first time the *Susie-Q* crew had fired a torpedo in combat, they didn't know that launching a torpedo — because it is lighter than a land bomb — would have little or no effect on a plane's flight path.

Susie-Q's crew began a battle for survival.

Trying to stay focused despite the uncertainty, Jim bit his still-unlit cigarette — and, he would realize later, he swallowed half.

Japanese gunners unleashed a barrage of flak. Jim steered *Susie-Q* downward, closer to the water. Then Ashley and Gogoj together yelled that a Zero was closing on their tail. Gogoj fired a burst from his turret gun. The Zero kept coming. Gogoj fired again, and "all hell broke loose," according to Melo. He heard Ashley yell he had been hit and saw the young South Carolina airman fall away from his gun.

Melo heard shells rake the fuselage. The gunfire hit the Plexiglass cover of the turret and blew it away from the plane, sending fragments that hit Gogoj. The gunner slumped, his face a mess of blood. Gogoj, whose hometown was Belrose, New York, assured fellow Long Islander Melo (from Astoria) that he wasn't badly hurt. Gogoj wrapped a rag around his forehead to keep blood out of his eyes and crawled back into the turret.

Melo scrambled back to the rear of the bomber to check on Ashley. He was in severe pain, his shot-up leg looking like hamburger. "Throw me out and end the agony," Ashley begged. Melo ignored the request and tried to call Muri, but the intercom was dead.

Susie-Q continued towards Akagi, the B-26 close to the water and so low she was below the carrier's flight deck. Japanese ships blasted all the lead and steel they could toward the plane.

Flying only a few hundred feet above the ocean, Muri jammed the throttle and worked the control yoke to position his plane for whatever might happen next. If the torpedo had launched and hit its target, it would damage or perhaps even sink *Akagi*, Nagumo's flagship.

It "seemed as though every ship ahead of us had burst into

flames, they were throwing up that much flak," Jim said later.

Jim still wasn't sure the torpedo released, but he had no time to think about that. *Akagi's* hulk loomed ahead, the deck lay above *Susie-Q's* course. What am I going to do? The thought crossed Jim's mind before he did the only thing he could do: pull the plane up and buzz right down the deck, in the view of an astonished Nagumo, commander of Kido Butai and the man who led the attack on Pearl Harbor.

Jim saw that *Akagi* was trying to evade not only his plane but also the other three B-26 bombers in what was no longer a diamond formation but a struggle for survival by the individual B-26s. He stayed focused on *Akagi*. The big ship turned from where it presented a broadside target to where it almost faced *Susie-Q* along a vertical, bow-to-stern line. So, with *Akagi* straight ahead and her anti-aircraft guns pointed outwards to sea, Jim did the only thing possible — he pointed his bomber toward the bow of the carrier.

Susie-Q roared toward *Akagi*, approaching her deck in the opposite direction from where planes returning to the carrier landed. Johnson opened fire from his cramped nose gunner spot, his barrage so intense the rest of the crew couldn't see him through the smoke. The crew now could see Japanese sailors running across *Akagi's* deck, unsure what would happen and how to protect themselves.

Pren Moore looked at Muri. Beads of sweat trickled down his forehead. A remnant of his unlit cigarette dangled from his mouth.

"For God's sake, Jim, pull up! Pull up!" Moore shouted.

At the last second, Jim pulled back on the yoke and willed *Susie-Q* to clear *Akagi's* bow and barrel the length of the carrier's deck.

As Muri buzzed the ship, he spotted Nagumo standing on the deck. The Japanese commander ducked to avoid death.

"From the time I went up over the bow and down the deck, I can honestly say I don't suppose we were 50 feet above the deck," Muri recalled. He flew so low, he said afterward, that had he put *Susie-Q*'s wheels down, he could have landed on *Akagi*'s deck.

Johnson continued strafing as *Susie-Q* buzzed the length of the carrier deck; his bullets or fire from Collin's plane killed two defenders. *Susie-Q*'s wings hit and sliced two radio transmitting antennas as the bomber zoomed down the deck, hampering the carrier's communications. Then, Jim's plane blazed skyward again. We've done our job, Melo thought to himself. Jim, however, knew his task was unfinished. He still needed to pilot a damaged plane back to safety. His life and the lives of six other men, three of them wounded, would depend on his ability to get things done, to return to Midway in a plane so shot up it would never fly again. *Susie-Q*'s first combat flight would be her last.

When Jim cleared *Akagi*'s deck, adversity continued. First, he had to outrun the last Zero fighters pursuing *Susie-Q*, then he had to find Midway in what had become a flying wreck.

Lieutenant W.W. Moore, the navigator, used the plane's compass to "shoot the sun" for a bearing that would take the airmen to Midway. That didn't give *Susie-Q* an easy route back to the base, though. To compensate, Jim flew in a box pattern, looking for any sign of the atoll in the vastness of the Pacific.

"Look!" someone shouted. "Smoke!"

Sure enough, a burning biblical pillar, the result of the Japanese attack about two hours earlier, rose into the sky. Jim flew toward the smoke.

He still had to exercise caution. A spark could ignite fuel escaping from tanks and turn the bomber into an inferno as it plummeted to the water. Crewman Gogoj, who Jim said looked like a "blood-soaked rag," transferred fuel into two tanks that had stayed sealed.

About then, Jim saw a Zero returning from its strafing of Midway. The Zero dived toward him.

"Oh, oh, we're done," Jim told his crew.

The Japanese plane drew alongside him, so close the pilots eyed each other. Jim thought of the service revolver he carried and said to himself, I could shoot, and I could hit him. He held off, and the Zero pulled away, perhaps because it was running out of gas.

While Jim Muri and Jim Collins continued looking for Midway and struggled to save their lives and those of their crew, the odds of survival appeared just as bleak for two Navy airmen flying nearby.

Chapter 11 - Survival ... barely

Albert Earnest and Harry Ferrier pinned their hopes of surviving Japanese fire and returning to Midway on a shot-up Navy torpedo bomber, the only one left of six Avengers that took off from Midway just before the B-26s did. Earnest piloted the plane, which had two crewmen, Jay Manning and a teenager named Harry Ferrier. Ferrier had lied about his age when he enlisted in the Navy on January 28, 1941. He said he was 17, the age when one could sign up, but he was 16. On June 4, 1942, his boyhood disappeared.

Japanese fighter planes attacked Earnest's Avenger, killing Manning, and a bullet hit Ferrier and knocked him unconscious for a while. When he came to, he could see blood pouring down his face from a hole in his skull, which was intact.

Earnest called Ferrier on the intercom, wanting to know if their torpedo got away. Ferrier checked the bomb bay, but found it filled with Manning's blood, which prevented the crewman from seeing whether or not the torpedo was there.

Meanwhile, *Susie-Q* closed in on Midway, so damaged that Muri had no room for error. He held the right aileron and left rudder and descended at an off-kilter angle. Jim knew he would have to land Susie-Q with most of the plane's weight on the right wheel because pressure on the mangled left wheel would have broken the landing gear and sent the plane cartwheeling to a fatal end.

Even Midway seemed to be his enemy — on his approach, Jim took fire from defenders who thought he might be an enemy.

"We're going in anyway, hydraulics or not," Jim told his crew, referring to the plane's ruined control systems.

Susie-Q touched down and leaned as Jim steadied the plane as best he could. She lurched left, and Muri and Johnson stomped on the brakes. That didn't help because they were too damaged to work.

Somehow, Jim kept the plane upright as it touched down at 100 mph. *Susie-Q* landed violently, roared and shook; the forces combined to break the instrument panel loose, sending it into the pilots' laps. Men already wounded, farther back in the plane, got a further battering before the aircraft stopped.

Earnest continued flying, and he and Ferrier looked for the base. Then the Navy airmen both spotted a column of black smoke — the same marker Jim's crew used to find Midway — on the horizon. Earnest flew toward the atoll and tried to make the runway. His hard landing caused a wing to dip and hit the runway, sending the Avenger into a ground loop that spun the plane to a stop in the sand.

Susie-Q landed just before Earnest did, and Muri was among the men who ran out to rescue the Avenger fliers. Jim pulled Harry out of the smashed plane and got the shocked teenager to safety. The Army pilot and the Navy airman went their separate ways, never dreaming that fate would bring them together again six decades later during a ceremony for World War II veterans in Washington, D.C.

By then, medics had arrived at a shredded *Susie-Q* to tend to the crew, but fliers first got to look over the machine that saved their lives. She was a wreck. Fuel dripped from tanks; hydraulic fluid and oil ran onto the ground; and the propeller blades were chewed up. A wing blasted by the barrage fell off, and the shot-up radio antenna didn't work. Bullet holes had pulverized the engines and shredded the navigator compartment. Blood covered the plane's interior.

Susie-Q's fliers counted bullet holes, and their tally reached more than 500 — for one half of the plane. Convinced of the beating their ship had taken, the crew stopped counting. Jeeps took the men to the hospital, and all survived, including Ashley, the most wounded, who received a year of medical care. But *Susie-Q* was a casualty. A ground crew towed the battered bomber to the edge of the Midway lagoon and gave her a push, sending her to an oceanic grave where *Susie-Q* may rest to this day.

Good news, that all aboard the planes flown by Jim Muri and Jim Collins survived the wrenching experience, reached the families of those 14 men. Not so fortunate were those aboard the B-26s flown by Watson and Mayes, who died at sea along with their 12 crewmen.

A letter exists that supports the general sense of dread and hope felt by family members and friends while they waited for final word on the fate of airmen shot down in the Pacific. Mabel Mayes, Herb's widow, wrote the letter, postmarked June 20, 1942, and sent it from Redwood City, California, to Alice in Riverside.

Mabel, pregnant then, acknowledged the near certainty that her B-26 pilot husband and his crew died in the Japanese onslaught at Midway, but she clung to the slim hope he and his men had survived.

"It just doesn't seem possible that such a thing could happen to Herb, and I still have hope he may be stranded someplace and will be found unless he was in the plane that crashed into the sea," she said, adding that Ensign George Gay, the only survivor of *Hornet's* Torpedo Squadron 8 suicidal attack against the Japanese fleet, saw the wreckage of that B-26 in the water.

Later accounts cemented the historical record showing it was Mayes' plane that hurtled across Akagai's deck into the Pacific, killing all aboard.

As she closed, Mabel seemed resigned to her husband's death. She asked Alice to confirm Jim's military APO address so she could write him and have Herb's clothes mailed to her.

The three-day Battle of Midway was underway; it would, at its conclusion, shift the tide of war in the Pacific from Japan to the United States and influence the outcome of World War II, both in the Pacific and in Europe.

Muri and Collins, in their action reports submitted two days after the battle, on June 6, 1942, said the attack on Akagi exposed weaknesses in the B-26s' weaponry and combined Army Air Force and Navy tactics used in the battle.

"I consider all guns to have been unsatisfactory during the entire fight," Collins wrote. He noted these deficiencies: both turret guns hung up; one tail gun stopped firing after its first burst; and motors would not pull ammunition through the tracks to either tail gun, forcing crews to work the mechanism by hand.

Collins advocated replacing .30-caliber guns placed at the side windows with .50-caliber ones, and supplying them with 100-round ammunition cans instead of the 30-round cans the planes originally carried.

The B-26s needed to be beefed up with at least four .50-caliber fixed guns in the wings plus a single or twin .50-caliber moveable gun in the planes' noses, Collins said.

"I believe that these guns are vitally necessary because no bomber is a match for a bunch of fighters and particularly so when the few guns it has won't shoot and the gunners have not had sufficient training to shoot them."

None of his crew was wounded, but Collins' plane was "considerably shot up" and had to crash land on the Eastern Island airstrip upon its return. Collins reflected on the loss of two B-26s from his group and all men aboard — 14 total — plus dozens of Navy and Marine torpedo planes shot down and many of their men dead and expressed his belief that a coordinated attack of dive bombers and level bombers would have been less costly.

Muri seconded his commander's critique. "The airplane does not have enough fire power from the front," he wrote, calling for additional fixed guns, which would have allowed him to capitalize on opportunities to shoot down Japanese fighter planes and helped him break through anti-aircraft fire on his approach to the carrier.

"Another vital necessity is support from fighter planes as well as dive bombers. We had none of this support at all," he reported.

B-26 gunners needed more training, according to Muri. Instead of the practice on the ground they received, they needed the skill gained by firing at a target being towed in the air. Also, the B-26s needed more defensive firepower than that afforded by their lone .50-caliber tail gun. *Susie-Q*'s tail gun jammed, and tail gunner Ashley was wounded in the fight, but the crew coped because co-pilot Pren Moore crawled from the front of the plane to the back and manned the tail gun.

Yes, the B-26 crews received hurried, inadequate torpedo training from the Navy in Hawaii before they headed to Midway. And the battle was their initiation into combat. But early reports that the B-26s, or the much-higher-flying B-17s that dropped bombs toward the Japanese fleet, made hits on enemy carriers

123

proved false. Muri, Collins, Mayes and Watson, pilots of the Midway Marauders, and their crews contributed to ultimate U.S. victory in ways other than sending torpedoes into the sides of carriers.

Although the Marauders missed the mark with their torpedoes, the military's top ranks noted the clear value of the planes in torpedo warfare. That recognition triggered jockeying for the planes after the battle, as evidenced by a Navy memo that referred to 18 B-26s that were to be withdrawn from Hawaii's defense. Crews were getting the planes ready to be ferried to the Southwest Pacific.

"Commander Naval Air Base Defense is assigning in training of the B-26 crews. B-26 aircraft are considered of greatly more value as torpedo planes than as bombers. In view of the urgent need for long range torpedo planes in the Hawaiian area, it is recommended that representation be made for 18 B-26 aircraft to remain in this area," the memo said.

Photos

R.P. Muri with (l-r) Bob, Andy, Toots and Jim, about 1926. All four children served in World War II. (Sylvia Saadati)

1FFA 1933 - Second row from bottom: Bill Muri, president; Jim Muri, 6th from left. (Branding Iron, school yearbook photo)

Custer County Cowboys football (1935) - Jim, #12, middle row.
(Branding Iron)

Best friends Hank Swartz and Jim Muri (front row, third from left and fourth from left) in CCHS aviation class during their senior year. (Branding Iron)

Hank Swartz in Riverside (undated).
(Sylvia Saadati)

Jim Muri at Chanute Field – 1936
(Sylvia Saadati)

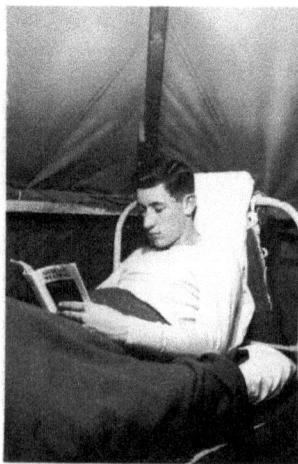
View of Chanute Field (left); Jim studying technical subjects at Chanute.
(Sylvia Saadati)

Randolph Field graduating class in 1941; Jim was a member of largest class in program history.
(Sylvia Saadati)

Top: A-26 dive bomber, the type of plane flown by Hank Swartz on his final mission. (National Museum of the Air Force, Dayton, Ohio) Bottom: Hank Swartz' Army Air Corps card. (Craig Swartz).

Jim (left) with Hank (center) and his father, visiting the friends in Riverside. (Sylvia Saadati)

Left: Midway Atoll in 1941. (from U.S. Navy Archives) Below: Jim (right) recovering from a ruptured appendix and appendectomy in a photo taken in early 1942 after he reached Hickam Field in Hawaii. His gaunt appearance alarmed his young wife, Alice.(Sylvia Saadati)

22nd airmen depart from March Field by train for San Francisco before boarding a Navy convoy that took them to Hawaii in February 1942. (Sylvia Saadati)

Clockwise, from top: Jim Muri in his B-26; Jim (left), Jo Jo Dewan, Herb Mayes (bottom); Jim (left) "horsing around" with fellow 22nd airmen. Bottom left: Jim, on rail, with John Augustine. (Sylvia Saadati)

View inside the flight deck of a B-26. (Screen shot from Cockpit 360 smartphone app)

B-26 carrying torpedo in flight.
(Navy archives)

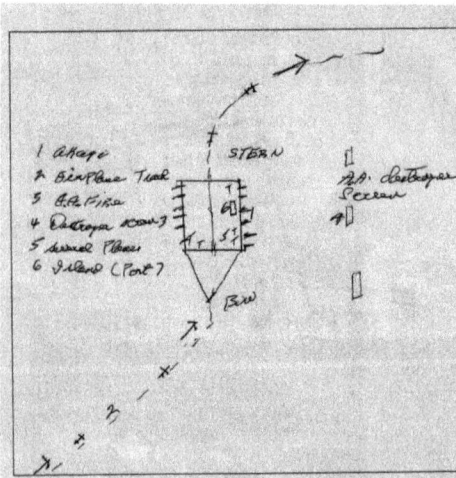

Jim's drawing of the attack on Akagi;
Distinguished Service Cross awarded by the Army
Air Force to Jim after the Battle of Midway.
(Sylvia Saadati, Joshua Muri)

Damage from the Japanese bombing of Midway: the pillar of smoke that Jim in his B-26 and Frank Earnest in his Navy Avenger used to find their way back to the base. (Navy archives)

Jim's two brothers who also were Army Air Force pilots: Bob (left), flew B-17 Flying Fortresses and was shot down over Germany; Andy flew B-24 Liberators in the Pacific. (Sylvia Saadati)

133

Clockwise from top: Jim with infant son, James, and Alice with James, at their home in Valparaiso, Florida, while Jim was stationed at Eglin Field; the Muri family in 1946. (Sylvia Saadati)

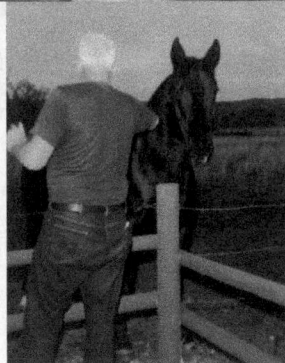

Clockwise, from top: Children in the Muri family gather around Jim to hear a story in 1957; Jim tends to a horse at Bridger Creek; "gone fishing" in one of the streams near the Bridger Creek place. (Sylvia Saadati)

Honors late in life

Top left - Jimmy Doolittle Award, presented to Jim Muri in Washington, D.C., in 2003; top right: Billings radio personality Lonnie Bell, who wrote "Midway": bottom – "old buddies," Jim Muri (left) and Joe Diviak, who first met at Chanute Field in 1936, reunited at the 2003 Doolittle Award ceremony. (Roger Nelson, Dennis Gaub, Roger Nelson)

His country says goodbye to a hero

Jim's 2013 burial in the Eastern Montana Veterans Cemetery in Miles City. An Air Force representative presents the ceremonial flag to his daughter, Sylvia, flanked (from left) by Roger Nelson; Jim's grandson, Joshua Muri and Jim's son, James Muri. (Roger Nelson)
Below – Jim's gravestone and Alice's gravestone at the Miles City Cemetery. (Dennis Gaub)

Chapter 12 - News of Victory Ripples Out

Some of the first major coverage of the battle appeared in the *New York Times*, which published a Page One story on June 6, 1942. Cabled from Pearl Harbor, the story appeared beneath a stack of headlines that told casual readers all they needed to know without reading further.

Across the top:

"Severe Damage Inflicted on Japanese Fleet in Battleships, Carriers, Cruisers, Transports; Foe Retires from Midway; Battle Continues."

Below that were smaller headlines that would have warmed Jim's heart had he gotten his hands on a copy of the newspaper.

"Our Fliers Excel."

"Foes' Losses 'Far Out of Proportion" to Ours in Battle," Nimitz Says."

"Carrier Torpedoed."

" 'Several Ships' in Each of Combat Classes of Enemy Are Hit."

Millions of Americans got to hear what Army Air Force pilots and crews, aboard B-26s and B-17s, accomplished at Midway ten days after the battle. On June 14, 1942, Honolulu radio station KGU linked with New York and contributed a twenty-minute segment about the battle to the national Army Hour broadcast. NBC carried the weekly program, which brought the voices and heroism of American servicemen from fronts around the world during the war.

Brig. Gen. Willis Hale, Army Air Force commander at Midway, took the microphone first.

"The Battle of Midway was primarily an air operation. From the time the enemy was first sighted by air reconnaissance until he turned and fled three days later, our combined Army, Navy and Marine fliers constantly pounded him from the skies, scoring hit after hit," he said in a report on the broadcast printed in the *Honolulu* (HI) *Star-Advertiser* (June 15, 1942).

Hale summarized the damage suffered by Yamamoto's fleet: "three or four of Japan's best carriers"; sure hits against "a couple of their battleships before they had fired a broadside"; and two cruisers and several destroyers and troop transports sent to the ocean bottom or damaged.

"The Battle of Midway definitely was a major defeat for the Japanese Navy," Hale said.

"It is not the final chapter in the Allied struggle in the Pacific, but it was a chapter written the way Americans wanted it written."

Next, listeners heard accounts from Lieutenant Colonel Brooke Allen, a B-17 pilot and squadron commander; Collins and the nose gunner/bombardier on his plane, Ernest Mohon; and Pren Moore, co-pilot of *Susie-Q*. Jim Muri wasn't on the broadcast, but he got ample recognition on the program.

Listeners heard that Jim's bomber "planted a fish (torpedo)" on *Akagi* – which turned out not to have happened, but Moore's description of the ordeal was accurate. He said Gogoj, despite being hit in the face, continued firing his turret gun, and *Susie-Q* toughed it out and saved the lives of her crew.

"Our plane was pretty badly shot up. The top edges of the wings looked like someone had gone over them with a meat chopper, and the gas tanks were shot up.

"Thanks to the bullet proofing and the expert maneuvering of

Lieutenant Muri, we got back to Midway. Even though our plane, old *Susie-Q*, had more than 500 bullet holes in her."

People back home stayed in the know even if they missed the Army Hour account or reports in leading national newspapers that gave Jim's flight prominent mention.

Detailed battle news, including the account of Jim's feat, reached Montana by late June 1942. His hometown newspaper, the *Miles City Star*, carried articles, as did newspapers elsewhere in Montana, such as the *Dillon Examiner* (southwestern region) and the *Big Timber Pioneer* (central region). Stories on June 25, 1942, in the *Examiner* and the *Pioneer* appeared under an identical headline: "Miles City Pilot Proves Big Headache to Japan."

Those articles began:

"Montana's fighting men are doing right by themselves in the business of taking the shine off the Rising Sun in the Pacific War.

"One of them in particular, James P. Muri, 23, of Miles City, helped give the Nipponese a mauling in the Midway Island battle and saw enough adventure in a few minutes to last him to a ripe old age." (Jim did, reaching 94 before his death in 2013.)

"Secretly trained torpedo plane crews, in their first action, plunged torpedoes into two of the Japanese carriers sunk in the battle." Word of Japan's resounding defeat trickled back to Montana, to people in the southeast corner of the state who knew Jim Muri, and individuals elsewhere for whom his name probably triggered memories of a star athlete at Custer County High School.

A wire service news report in the *Big Timber Pioneer* (and picked up by other newspapers in the state) on July 2, 1942, bore the headline: "Jap Defeat Worse Than First Reported." It said the Navy waited until it had a complete set of battle reports, and

141

verified them, before detailing the American triumph.

The tally of ships sunk included all four Japanese carriers positioned to strike Midway, two heavy cruisers, three destroyers and a cargo transport vessel. Japan's deaths totaled at least 18,000, the account said.

More conservatively, on June 10, the Navy said two, possibly three, Japanese carriers and one other ship, a destroyer, had gone to the bottom. The Japanese, meanwhile, put on a brave face and acknowledged only the loss of a carrier.

Equally important to Japan's fate as the war continued, Midway cost the country 275 planes and their skilled pilots, many among the best in the world when conflict began.

A United Press reporter went to Miles City, Jim's hometown throughout high school, and found his grandmother, beaming with pride, at her home. The wire-service reporter wrote an article published nationally, which described Mary Johnson as a "tanned, old, white-haired woman" standing in the doorway of her log house (*Great Falls Tribune*, June 14, 1942).

"Why of course we're proud of him, but then we've been proud of him all the time," Mrs. Johnson said.

The UP reporter talked to other Miles City residents who called the Muris "the kind of people who have made this country what it is today."

The article said the Miles City community got a hint of fame to come for a native son a month earlier. People identified "Jimmy" as the officer who appeared in the cover picture of the May 16, 1942, issue of a national magazine, which showed Air Corps members preparing for their next flight.

(It's unclear which national magazine carried Jim's photo on its cover. Family members say it may have been *Life* or *Look* magazine, both widely circulated publications that pioneered photojournalism. *Colliers*, another magazine in wide circulation, may have carried the photo. Research in the Montana State University library archives of these magazines did not produce the cover photo.)

Meanwhile, news of Muri's feat trickled Down Under to his fellow fliers in the 22nd who had continued on to Australia, including his friend Jo Jo Dewan. Given wartime censorship and the sometimes muddled nature of communications, it's not surprising that Dewan's diary entry for July 22, 1942, contains errors of fact.

Dewan started that day by mentioning that he wrote letters to his wife, Elsie, and to Muri and got them on a B-24 Liberator flying to the U.S. that night. He continued:

"Just heard all about Jim being in the Midway Battle and sinking an aircraft carrier. He and another plane got one carrier between the two of them. Not bad. Quite some kid! I heard he had most of his crew killed, too."

On the evening of August 29, 1942, Dewan and his companions dined at a "little French cafe" in the town, then went to the movies. Movies then included a newsreel, short film footage of the top news of the day, before the feature film. What two 22nd members saw that evening hit home.

"And in the newsreel we saw none other than James P. Muri!" he wrote. "I was so surprised I nearly fell out of my seat!

"He had grown a mustache, and looked very funny — and talked with (his) usual 90 mile-an-hour speed. He was telling about his crash landing at Midway Island. It tickled Junior (Lt. Norman

143

Hall) and me to see old Jim. How I'd like to see the old soak! Our hero!!!"

At about the same time, on the other side of the globe, Jim's family in Carterville — his parents and younger brothers and sisters — experienced the same thrill as Dewan and Hall. The operator of a theater in nearby Miles City, knowing a Midway battle newsreel had arrived with the feature film showing at his movie house, had a driver go to the Muri ranch, pick up the family members and bring them to Miles City to see the newsreel. (A clip of the newsreel was available on YouTube when this was written.)

A few days later, on September 3, 1942, sad news arrived at the 22nd camp in the Australian bush, although Dewan prefaced that with good cheer.

"It was good to get back to camp and see all the boys again. Johnny Miller was here — arrived from Hawaii. He brought news, of all sorts," Dewan said.

Part of the news was that Jim had gotten back to the states. He was at Wright Field in Dayton, Ohio. Dewan didn't know it then, but Jim and Alice Muri stopped there as they drove to Washington, D.C., on Jim's classified courier mission to deliver secret documents to Army headquarters.

Dewan continued ticking off names of 22nd fliers positioned across the Pacific.

"Pete Moore (Muri's co-pilot at Midway in Susie-Q), (Paul) Pollock, 'Chunky' Keith (Chambliss Keith), R.O. Miller — are all at Wheeler Field in Hawaii in their B-26s."

Then a punch to Dewan's gut.

"Herb Mayes was killed in the Midway Battle — along with his crew of (Lt. Gerald) Barnacle, (co-pilot, Lt. Garnett) McAllister and (Lt. Billy) Hargis, navigator, and rest of crew.

"This last bit of news shocked me to my heels. Herb — one of my best friends. Poor Mabel (Mayes), and they were so marvelous to Elsie — and Herb's folks were, too."

It didn't take long for word of the battle to reach Riverside, and the news about her husband's Midway feat evoked mixed emotions, most prominent being surprise and pride, in Jim's young wife.

When Alice wrote to Jim, he was back in Hawaii, recovering from the psychological stress of his experience. He phoned Alice soon after the battle. Alice replied with a letter dated June 14, 1942.

"I had no idea when you called last weekend the wonderful and dangerous thing you had done," she said.

As word of the U.S.'s epic victory trickled back to the mainland, newspaper reporters looked up Alice at a "fast and furious" rate.

"There isn't a person in the world any prouder than I am," she said. Yet, mixed with pride, Alice said she was praying Jim would not have to do more "guinea pig work." That was a clear allusion to his bomber and the other B-26s being sent into battle with torpedoes instead of bombs, the primary weapon of the aircraft; the almost complete lack of torpedo training the B-26 pilots and crewmen received before the mission; and, foremost, Jim's improvised tactic of survival that involved buzzing *Akagi*'s deck.

"It seems far more dangerous than your ordinary work," Alice said.

She was shocked at hearing about the death of Mayes, Jim's fellow 22nd Group pilot, and his crew.

Jim and Alice had become friends with Mayes and his wife, a Stanford University graduate and teacher pregnant with the couple's first child at the time of Herb's death. Alice asked Jim to fill her in on the other men who perished when Mayes' airplane was shot down.

By the time Alice wrote, dozens of newspapers had published a picture of *Susie-Q's* nameplate, the only thing salvaged when servicemen pushed the B-26, shredded with more than 500 bullet holes and considered an unsalvageable wreck, into the Midway lagoon. Jim, however, missed that photo session, and his phone call relieved Alice.

"Darling, when I hear about what happened, I wish I had you safely here at home. I know you will be coming home to me and all the proud Muris and Moyers soon, but, Ducky, you don't call that exactly being careful, do you?"

She qualified her concern by saying Jim's ability to safely fly *Susie-Q* back to Midway, with wounded crewmen on board, proved he was careful and "a wonderful pilot."

The aura from the U.S. triumph in the Pacific, and Jim's vital role in the outcome, extended to the Bank of America office where Alice worked for a man named Harris.

"Mr. Harris is as tickled as a little boy about the whole thing. ... [He] told everyone who came into the office that his secretary had 'wings' on her feet today. When they asked why, he gave them the whole story as far as we know it."

Acknowledging that she might be selfish, Alice said she wished Jim could get a furlough. That would allow the couple to "get a cabin and stay in the hills away from people and the war for a week or two anyway."

Alice voiced steadfast affection for Jim.

"I love you so much that when I think of what you've been

through and knowing how you feel about Herb and the boys makes me cry inside, and it's so much worse when you can't shed tears."

Alice reminded Jim to take care of himself and closed by asking him to phone her whenever he could. The last call "was only $8, and that ain't much," she said.

Jim found it difficult to handle the battle aftermath. In a June 26, 1942, letter to Alice, he said he was "in the dumps" and had gotten no mail since before he flew *Susie-Q* to Midway on May 29.

Then he sounded a positive note.

"Incidentally, dearest, we have all been recommended for the D.S.C. Distinguished Service Cross. It is the next highest honor the Govt. can give. I hope it goes through as I certainly would be a proud boy," he said.

Jim told Alice his superiors had recommended him for promotion to captain, another point of understandable pride.

"I don't know when this will all come through but it should be in the next year or two," he said with obvious sarcasm.

Publicity and fame were headed Jim's way. An unnamed general had called him to set up an interview the following day. Jim didn't know what the subject was, "but you can bet your life I'll do some tall talking."

He asked his wife to save the copy of *Life* magazine that had an article about him because he wouldn't get to see it in Hawaii. Also, he asked her to keep an issue of *Collier's* magazine that mentioned him. He didn't provide dates for either article.

Letters between Jim, in Hawaii, and Alice, in Riverside, may have crossed in the mail or been delayed because Jim's next letter on June 29 refers to Alice's June 14 letter that reached him when he got to Hickam Field from Midway.

"Very old to say the least, but [the letter] was worth its weight in gold. It made me very happy to see a letter from my wife and dearest," Jim said.

Then he showed his amazement at being in line for the top award the Army can give.

"I was very fortunate in having dinner with Gen. Hale the other night, at which time he told me that my crew and I are all going to receive the Distinguished Service Cross in a couple of days.

"Gee, honey, can you imagine that? Who ever thought I could get such a thing? I still don't believe it."

Hale said the Army had already order DSC medallions and citations from Washington, so Jim knew the news was true.

"Darling, I don't think you realize how happy your little Jimmy is," he said, adding that he expected his promotion to captain to come through by August 1.

"Darling, you said no one could help loving me. I wonder about that. The way about 30 boatloads of Japs were shooting at me, I was sure they were trying to injure me or else they were damn mad at one of the boys in the crew."

Jim and the other Marauder men received official acclaim for what they accomplished at Midway in July 1942. Lt. Gen. Delos C. Emmons, acting on behalf of President Franklin Roosevelt, awarded the Distinguished Service Cross to the twenty-eight officers and airmen in Captain Jim Collins' squadron. The DSC is the Army's highest honor and second only to the Medal of Honor — awarded by the president in Congress' name — in the pantheon of U.S. military laurels.

An article in the *Baltimore* (MD) *Sun* (July 11, 1942), noted that some awards were posthumous. Every honoree participated in the first torpedo bomber attack carried out by the Army, the paper said.

The Army commended Collins, the flight commander, for "extraordinary heroism in action near Midway June 4." The Meridian, Mississippi, airman led a successful attack against Japanese warships in the face of heavy Zero fighter plane and ship anti-aircraft fire, according to his citation.

"Captain Collins sought out a large enemy aircraft protection, protected on all sides by gunfire of all types from enemy battleships, cruisers and destroyers" and "carried out his most hazardous mission under the most adverse conditions."

Jim's citation said he "participated in an extremely hazardous and difficult torpedo-bombing mission against the Japanese Navy. He displayed extraordinary heroism and courageousness in maneuvering his airplane to secure the maximum effectiveness of his torpedo in the face of superior enemy fighter and anti-aircraft opposition, and was highly instrumental in the success of the first torpedo attack ever carried out by the Army Air Forces.

"The personal courage and zealous devotion to duty displayed by First Lieutenant Muri on this occasion have upheld the highest traditions of the military service and reflect great credit upon himself, the Far East Air Force, and the United States Army Air Forces."

Besides Muri and Collins, those mentioned in the *Sun's* incomplete list of DSC honorees — all cited for heroism and skill — included:

From Susie-Q

- Second Lieutenant Russell H. Johnson, Chicago

- First Lieutenant P.L. "Pren" Moore, El Centro, California, co-pilot, cited for "leaving his station to administer to the wounds of three wounded members of his crew and manning a gun position whose gunner was totally disabled and fighting off enemy fighters"

- Staff Sergeant John J. Gogoj, Bellerose, Long Island, New York, aerial engineer and gunner, who fought off "enemy fighters and although he incurred painful head wounds continued to operate his gun until free of enemy opposition"

- Corporal Frank L. Melo, Astoria, Long Island, New York, and Private Earl D. Ashley, Williamston, South Carolina, two other gunners who kept firing despite being wounded

From other B-26s

- Second Lieutenant Gerald J. Barnacle, Pittsfield, Massachusetts

- Second Lieutenant Colin O. Villenes, Chicago

- Second Lieutenant William S. Watson, Dixon, Illinois

- Second Lieutenant Thomas Weeks, Jr., Model Tennessee

- Technical Sergeant Raymond S. White, Altoona, Pennsylvania

- Sergeant Albert E. Owen, Grand Island, Nebraska

- Corporal John D. Joyce, Taylor, Pennsylvania

Jim's letter in early July 1942 alerted Alice to the physical and psychological toll the battle had taken on him. He said he had lost ten pounds and hadn't been able to sleep; an earlier letter said medics gave him sleeping pills but they didn't help.

Jim had shaved off the Errol Flynn-style mustache he and his crew members grew on Midway. The reason for having the mustache — to distinguish themselves from Navy fliers while flying a mission under Navy command — was gone, so why keep whiskers?

He asked Alice to not hold false hope for his quick return home. The base commander had called and told Muri and his men to pack their bags for likely duty in Australia with the rest of the 22nd Group.

Jim asked for news of his brothers Bob and Andy; their father, R.P. Muri, knew they had joined "something" but hadn't been told he had two more sons training to becoming Army pilots.

Jim told Alice he got a letter from the older of his two sisters, Marie, better known as "Toots." When she saw the newsreel in the summer of 1942 that showed her brother as a Midway hero, she was shocked because she hadn't seen Jim in three years. Toots would follow her brothers' path of service to country by becoming an Army nurse later in the war.

Chapter 13 - Torpedo Trainer

With the Battle of Midway over, Jim began the non-combat part of his military career, which brought challenges different from when fire from Japanese planes and ships pummeled his plane.

In late June or early July 1942, Jim Muri returned to the mainland, his rest-and-recovery at Oahu after the battle finished. He went to Riverside and picked up Alice, who had been working as a secretary at a Bank of America branch office while the Army stationed him in the Pacific.

"Let's go, honey," Jim said to his wife of six months. "I've got to head back to Washington, D.C., but it's time to see some of this country before we get there. Plus, I want you to meet my folks and my brothers and sisters in Montana."

So, the young couple — he would turn 24 that October, and Alice had just celebrated her 21st birthday — took off on a cross-country car trip. Their destination was Army headquarters in the capital, where Jim had to deliver a briefcase locked to his wrist. The only time he could rid himself of the briefcase was when he slept at night or showered, and even then, the briefcase had to remain in his immediate possession, according to Army orders. To this day, it's unknown what the briefcase contained, but it's likely Jim was a courier delegated to deliver eyes-only documents to headquarters.

The Army issued Jim a service revolver to carry on his person for the trip. That posed a problem at one point. The Muris drove through Yellowstone National Park on their way to the Carterville, home of Jim's parents. When they reached a park entrance gate, a ranger noticed the loaded pistol that Jim carried.

"Firearms not allowed; you can't bring that into the park, sir," the ranger said, likely unaware he was addressing a serviceman awarded the Distinguished Service Cross.

Jim thought quickly. He found a note in his wallet and produced what he needed: a phone number for Army headquarters. "Here, call this number," he said to the ranger. "They'll tell you I'm on official business, and the Army has ordered me to carry this pistol."

The phone call made, Jim and Alice got the green light to enter the park, where they became tourists and sightseers in the world's first national park. Thus, they enjoyed an experienced shared by millions of people around the globe in the almost 150 years since Congress created Yellowstone in 1872.

After their visit to Eastern Montana, the Muris continued on to the capital after a stop in Dayton, Ohio. They waited there for a while; Jim thought he would be sent to Australia to rejoin the 22nd Bomb Group members dispatched to Hawaii with him in February 1942. But the Army had other plans for the now famous Montanan.

"I had orders back to the states on a classified courier mission to Dayton, Ohio, and then Washington, D.C., and when I got to Washington, they were just in the process of starting the torpedo school at Eglin Field. Being a person who dropped a torpedo out at Midway, they figured I would be a logical candidate and go down there and give them a hand, which I did," he said, recalling decades later events that happened in the summer of 1942..

The Army orders sent Jim and Alice driving down the Atlantic Coast to Florida.

Jim reported to the torpedo training school — officially, in Army speak, the First Torpedo Proving Ground — at Eglin Field. The story among Muri family members goes that Gen. Henry

"Hap" Arnold, chief of the Army Air Forces, valued what Muri had done as pilot of *Susie-Q*, equipped with a torpedo that he launched at the Japanese carrier *Akagi*, and Arnold wanted the young flier where he could impart his torpedo knowledge to other Army pilots. So, a role as an instructor, rather than further combat duty, was the next step on Muri's military career path.

When Jim and Alice arrived in Florida, they became part of a massive migration fueled by wartime military needs. The 1940 census counted 1.9 million residents in the state; the population grew to 2.8 million in 1950.

Thanks to base construction and related infrastructure projects, Florida's economy boomed during the war years. The military built more than 200 bases from the late 1930s through 1945, and all those facilities needed roads. The state added 1,560 miles of highway, which cost more than $44 million, from 1940 through 1944. By the time peace came, Florida changed from a rural state to one where urban residents could drive on more than 8,000 miles of paved roads.

A military airfield that sprung up almost overnight awaited Jim and Alice when they got to the Florida panhandle in September 1942. That facility, Eglin Field, got its start in 1933 as the Valparaiso Municipal Airport, a 137-acre facility with no paved runways or outbuildings. In March 1935, local officials received a federal grant to pave the airport runways and build barracks and a mess hall. Later that year, the airport, now 1,460 acres larger, took on a new identity as the Valparaiso Bombing and Gunnery Base.

The base got its lasting name on August 4, 1937, when the Army renamed it Eglin Field in honor of Lt. Col. Frederick Eglin, a flier killed in a plane crash.

Eglin grew rapidly as war clouds appeared on the horizon. In 1939, the Army Air Corps decided to use Eglin as a proving ground for aircraft armaments. The War Department got the needed room for that function by absorbing the Choctawhatchee National Forest, comprising 340,890 acres spread across three counties. The Air Corps also declared 4,000 square miles of the Gulf of Mexico part of Eglin Field for maneuvers.

A variety of Army units to train pilots came under the Eglin umbrella in the short time before Pearl Harbor. This expansion included the Air Corps Proving Ground, later the Proving Ground Command, activated on May 5, 1941. Jim later became part of this unit as commander of the torpedo training school. He thus became part of Eglin's development into one of the primary Army Air Force bases of World War II; it keeps significance today as Eglin Air Force Base.

The Muris settled in Valparaiso (named after the city of the same name in Indiana), which was about 10 miles from the gate to the airfield.

Jim and Alice moved into a community on edge because of an event that grabbed national headlines about two months before they arrived: a foiled plot to use German submarines to land Nazi saboteurs, U.S. citizens trained in Germany, on Long Island and Florida's Atlantic Coast so they could damage or destroy U.S. defense plants.

The young military couple picked up the vibrations, the sense of unseen threat in the air. Their daughter, Sylvia Saadati, described the times before she was born based on stories she heard from her parents.

"When they first got to Florida, they lived out in the boonies.

Their house was isolated. There were other homes further out, and they were told that known German sympathizers lived in some of those homes," she said.

Those thoughts, founded or not, took hold when Florida residents read a sensational news story on June 29, 1942. FBI Director J. Edgar Hoover reported that a German sub landed four saboteurs on shore at Ponte Vedra Beach on the night of June 17, according to the *Tampa* (FL) *Tribune* (June 29, 1941). The resort community, located south of Jacksonville, adjoined a six-mile stretch of beach, hardly any of it settled. Nearby was another almost uninhabited beach that stretched 30 miles to St. Augustine.

News of the enemy in their midst put Floridians on edge and prompted authorities to take measures to prevent further landing of saboteurs. Later that summer, Florida beaches were closed to nighttime use at the request of Army Gen. E.A. Evans, according to the *Tampa* (FL) *Times* (August 1, 1942).

Evans, commander of the Army's Florida sector, said his request applied to all beaches on the east and west coasts of the state, even privately owned ones and beaches in front of Gulf of Mexico hotels. He said the military had patrolled Florida's long coastline for some time, looking for enemy landings.

The general said he was asking for voluntary compliance, hoping that people would stay off the beaches at night, but "if that doesn't work that work, we'll enforce it."

Meanwhile, Valparaiso was struggling to meet the influx of Army airmen (and some women) assigned to Eglin. On September 5, 1942, officials in the town broke ground for 40 new homes, according to the *Pensacola* (FL) *News Journal* (September 6, 1942). The houses, intended to be rentals and subject to government rent

157

controls, were bungalows that overlooked the Gulf. They had five or six rooms with attached garages and were built as frame structures with asbestos siding and composition shingles.

The homes were equipped with electric ranges, refrigerators and heating units. Plans called for landscaped lots of 75 by 150 feet, with trees, shrubbery and grass, and room for gardens.

Alice Muri got a sense of what was going on at Elgin because the house she and Jim lived in was close to Choctawhatchee Bay. Thus, she could see Army airmen practicing in their planes and maneuvering over the water.

Sometimes, Alice saw small private planes flying across the bay. She may have assumed they were leisure flyers, but they weren't — they were part of the U.S. defense against German attacks by water.

The federal government started the Volunteer Civil Aeronautics Patrol, or "Flying Minute Men," as the organization became known, early in the war. The Army and Navy were short of planes for shore patrol duty. So, building on an idea that a World War I pilot, Gill Robb Wilson, brought to Air Force Chief Arnold, the CAP came into being. It grew to include about 80,000 people who helped with patrol duty and other defense-related tasks.

"The civilian pilots of the C.A.P. in their private planes, mostly little puddle-jumpers, undertook to spot Hitler's arrogant sea invaders and help to change the picture," Arnold said in his 1949 autobiography.

Few of the CAP pilots had ever flown across large bodies of water in their low-speed, short-range Piper Cubs and similar planes, "but now they were doing it, both men and women, with marked success," growing more expert and more enthusiastic, all for a per diem payment of eight dollars to cover their expenses.

Arnold asked Wilson if he thought CAP pilots would object to carrying bombs on their planes.

"Where do we get them?" Wilson replied.

Hence, the Army Air Force built special bomb racks at its depots for the CAP planes and outfitted them with inexpensive bombsights that made them ready to help the war effort.

"Thereafter, most of the C.A.P. planes carried bombs — fifty pounders the pilots could drop on the submarines, knowing full well if they were taken prisoner in civilian clothes, they would not be considered part of our armed forces, but guerrillas," Arnold wrote in his autobiography.

By the time the war ended, the CAP pilots had flown more than 24 million miles, mostly in single-engine planes over the ocean. They performed other tasks — for example, courier service, spotting forest fires and locating lost planes.

The CAP provided an additional benefit, Arnold said, by providing "a reservoir of cadets and enlisted men for the Army Air Forces. They did a magnificent job all through the war, and they did sink some submarines."

Seeing military and civilian planes over the bay did not, however, ease the loneliness Alice experienced at home while Jim was at Eglin. He needed to drive their only car to work, so unless Alice became a girlfriend of other nearby military wives who had cars, she was stuck at home during her husband's working hours.

It wasn't an idyllic time, despite Florida's image then and now as a land of sunshine-drenched beaches, a playground for those who fled snowy northern states either in winter or for good.

Because of the known German sympathizers who lived in the

area and vermin — "the animal kind" in the yard, Saadati said — the Muris kept rifles in the house. The couple placed a firearm by each window, within easy reach in case they needed a gun. Also, when someone stepped outside, it was wise for them to check for snakes that might have curled up next to the door.

Jim and Alice's first house in Florida lacked basics such as locks on the doors and possibly window screens. Military development at a rapid pace resulted in a housing crunch — there weren't enough rentals available, and those on the market often lacked what are now considered necessities.

A kitchen and living room took up most of the first floor of the Muris' two-story house, and the bedroom was upstairs. The Muris had no children when they came to Eglin.

This was the setting for a story that Sylvia heard later and which she retold:

"Dad had come home. It was payday. They got paid in cash. He came in, and as he walked through the door, he said, 'The eagles screamed,' and he threw the money (paper bills with an eagle insignia) in the air.

" 'Good news; we've got money now,' " Jim said.

Alice picked up the bills and stacked them on a buffet table in the living room. The Muris finished their evening and went to bed. They maintained the routine had developed after Jim returned from Midway, when the intensity of his battle experience — having his plane pulverized, having three crewmen wounded, and suffering the shock of losing 14 colleagues, airmen on the two B-26s shot down over the Pacific — appeared to have inflicted lasting psychological wounds on Jim. In World War II, that condition became known as combat shock. Today, it's labeled post-traumatic stress disorder, the term Saadati prefers; her brother, James, says what his father felt might be called "survivor's guilt," stemming from his emotions about escaping the fate that befell the other Marauder men at Midway.

"They had this thing worked out if there was a problem (at night when they were asleep). My dad was really hard to wake up without him becoming violent. That was part of his PTSD; from the time I was a kid, he was still that way," Sylvia said.

"They had this system worked out between the two of them that if something was wrong and they had to wake the other, they needed to be quiet about it. They would reach over and grab the other person on the wrist or the hand and, without making noise, squeeze really hard until the other person woke up."

Alice woke one night, certain she heard someone in their home.

"She reached over and grabbed hold of my dad. He came awake right away."

Jim whispered, " 'What is it? And she said, 'Somebody is downstairs,'" according to Sylvia.

To see if there was an intruder, the Muris had to tiptoe down the stairs and then walk across the living room, which had a wooden floor, to reach the light switch on the far side of the room.

Chuckling at the image as she related the incident in 2019, Sylvia said, "My dad gets up in his jammies and he says, 'Stay here.' She says, 'No!' She grabs hold of his shirt tail. She's not about stay up there alone. They're going down the stairs as quietly as possible — I'm sure they were wooden, creaking — going ... carefully and sneakily, not knowing what they're going to find down there because it was obvious somebody was in the house."

When Jim reached the bottom of the stairs, he scurried across the living room and flipped the light switch on. Nobody was there.

"So, they started looking around. The person who had been in the house didn't even touch the money that was on the buffet. They don't know what the person was in there for. Were they just reconning the place to see what kind of things might be there or what?" Sylvia said.

The guns were also untouched, yet the episode troubled the Muris enough to prompt them to seek other housing.

"Whatever it was, it sure as heck spooked them. And, of course, my dad didn't want her staying out there by herself too much," Saadati said.

The episode made her parents hunt for another home, but "they weren't to be had. They had too much military at that time and not enough houses to rent."

As Jim and Alice settled in to life at Eglin, the saboteur saga continued. A trial by a military commission found six of the men who landed on the Atlantic Coast by submarine guilty of treason; they were executed by electric chair in Washington, D.C., on August 8, 1942. Officials held the men's bodies in Walter Reed Hospital for some time to allow relatives or friends to claim them. No one did, and the men were buried in what a photo caption in the *Washington Evening Star* said was a potter's field; the photo appeared in the *Pensacola News Journal* (October 15, 1942). Unpainted wooden tombstones, bearing numbers, not names, marked their graves.

What was called the biggest treason trial in U.S. history began in Chicago in the fall of 1942. Three Chicago couples, relatives and friends of one of the men executed in August, Herbert Hans Haupt, were put on trial. All were German-born naturalized citizens who had been in the country more than 15 years, the *Tampa Tribune* reported (October 26, 1942). They faced charges of "41 overt actions of violating the constitution in its only reference to a criminal offense, treason," the paper said.

A witness' testimony rocked the trial. Jurors heard that Haupt had worked for a Chicago company that manufactured one of the most secret weapons of the war, the Norden gunsight, used for precision bombing in military planes. The government witness, manager of the Simpson Optical Co., said Haupt and another man worked for the firm until May 1941, when both left the U.S. for Germany, where the Nazis trained them for sabotage and returned them to the U.S. with a sleuth landing in the summer of 1942, according to the *Pensacola News Journal* (October 31, 1942).

Proceedings against the individuals charged in Chicago with treason dragged on for two years. Mrs. Erna Haupt, Herbert Haupt's mother, was ordered to appear before the Enemy Alien Board in September 1942, said a report in the *Richmond* (IN) *Palladium-Item* (September 14, 1944). A federal judge filed nolle prosse charges against her in July on condition she give up her U.S. citizenship and go to prison. (Nolle prosse is a legal term that means a legal action has been entered on the record saying the prosecutor will proceed no further in a criminal or civil case.) The court sentenced her husband, Hans Max Haupt, to life imprisonment during his second treason trial in 1944.

Muri's flight log for July 1942 contains interesting, hard-to-explain information. It lists him as a first lieutenant — he was — but as part of the "Air Reserve." That designation puzzles Sylvia, who doesn't think her father ever was on wartime reserve status.

Also, for July 1942, Muri's flight log shows him as attached to

163

the 7th Bomber Command, 58th Bomber Group. Logs have a line for "station," that is, the field or base from which a pilot flew that month. That line is empty. All the log says is that Muri got 20 hours and 25 minutes of flight time that month, all on local flights.

His log is missing pages for August 1942. By September, he's shown as part of the First Torpedo Proving Ground Squadron at Eglin. He racked up nine hours of flight time that month, all while piloting B-26s.

Jim settled into his new role as commander of the torpedo training school, and in 1943, he and Alice moved into a home at 414 Chicago Avenue in Valparaiso. It met their desire to bring Alice out of her previous rural isolation and to a place with neighbors nearby. While they lived there, their first child, James, was born on December 25, 1943. His father had been promoted to major by then, so friends called the Muri's toddler the Major's Minor.

A white picket fence surrounded the new home, where trees and a grassy lawn grew instead of the sandy yard the Muris had at their previous home because of its closeness to the bay. The couple now could take in recreational life at the base, which was highlighted by music, sports, and book reading.

In the winter of 1944, servicemen and families of the married men heard a concert at the Devilliers Street USO Club. The 30-piece 727th United States Army Band of Eglin Field, activated in March 1943, played classics and numbers from "The Music of the Masters," according to the *Pensacola News Journal* (February 27, 1944). Half the members were former professional musicians.

Also, the Walton High School Key Club presented a minstrel at Eglin that was "really appreciated — if applause may be taken as a token of appreciation," the *News Journal* reported (February 27, 1944).

Service teams that played major sports were a staple of military bases in World War II, including Eglin. It didn't have a football team in 1942 but was expected to be well-represented in basketball, the *News Journal* said (October 15, 1942).

By 1943, Jim's athletic skills, put to use by the Army, gained national attention. Newspapers across the country, including the *Casper* (WY) *Star-Tribune* (June 18, 1943) carried this wire-service report of his sports feats:

"Major James P. Muri, 24-year-old commander of the Wildcat Squadron at Eglin Field, Fla., doesn't appear to be any prouder of the Distinguished Service Cross he received for sinking a Jap aircraft carrier than he is of the Wildcats' athletic achievement." That wasn't surprising, readers were told, because Muri was an all-state football and basketball player in high school in Miles City. Jim's prep skills carried over and helped the Wildcats win every sports tournament and league title at Eglin.

In November 1943, Eglin Field's Red Cross director issued a call for Pensacola residents to donate books for men at Eglin, many in isolated spots. He said Eglin men, far from amusement at large population centers, craved reading material, especially fiction books.

"Let's not fail on this appeal. Prove Pensacola's deep interest in the men in service," the Red Cross official told the *News Journal* (November 2, 1943).

Chapter 14 - A POW Brother

War got personal for Jim in late winter 1944 when he learned enemy fire had shot down the brother behind him in the family line during a bombing run over Germany, and his sibling was being held as a prisoner of war.

That brother was Robert (Bob), who enlisted in the Army Air Force in 1942, at the same time as the trailing brother, Andy, two years younger than Robert and four years younger than Jim. Bob and Andy trained at Williams Field, Arizona, before being deployed overseas, according to the Missoula, Montana, *Missoulian* (March 1944). Andy flew B-24 Liberators in the Southwest Pacific, and the Army awarded him the Distinguished Flying Cross for his service.

Robert's assignment to the European Front took him to England, where he became a B-17 pilot. Sometimes he flew as co-pilot, which was the situation on February 24, 1944, when his Flying Fortress went down over Germany between Talge and Badbergen. His operations officer, Lt. Col. Robert C. Williams, later declared Bob missing in action.

Norwood Garrett piloted the heavy bomber on which Bob shared command duties the day the plane came down behind enemy lines. Garrett, Bob and their nine crew members took off from the Royal Air Force's Thurleigh Station, according to an April 28, 2019 email from Sylvia Saadati containing material compiled by Sue Moyer of the 306th Bombardment Group Facebook page. The men were part of the 423rd Bombardment Squadron, within the 306th BG.

Bob's bomber took part in Operation Argument, a series of raids by the USAAF and the RAF Bomber Command from

February 20-25, 1944. The Big Week, as the massive operation is known, was part of the European strategic bombing campaign against Nazi Germany's aircraft industry. Allied planners designed the operation to lure the Luftwaffe into a decisive battle to damage the German Air Force so severely that the Allies would gain air superiority. This would ensure success when they invaded Europe, a goal accomplished during Operation Overlord when American and British troops under the command of General Dwight Eisenhower landed on the beaches of Normandy on D-Day, June 6, 1944

Its Big Week performance earned the 306th its second Distinguished Unit Citation. The group got its first DUC for a Jan. 11, 1944, attack on aircraft factories in central Germany, carried out without fighter escort in the face of strong opposing forces.

It didn't take long for word of Robert's fate to reach R.P. and Nellie Muri, who by 1944 had three sons serving as Army Air Force pilots. Jim, stationed in Eglin, did everything he could to find out more about what happened to Bob. He sent at least two telegrams to his parents.

On March 12, 1944, Jim wrote: "Dear Mom. Don't worry too much. Probably was not as bad as it seems. Chances are great he is alive. Air mail to follow."

In his telegram on April 15, 1944, Jim said: "Letter from Bob's CO (commanding officer) encouraging. He had every opportunity to bail out as the ship was under control. When last seen, he was (illegible) which is very encouraging. (Illegible) to follow."

A letter from Montana Senator Burton Wheeler to R.P. and Nellie Muri contained a human touch.

"Mrs. Wheeler joins me in the hope that the war may end soon and (Bob) will be with you once more. We offer our heartfelt sympathy in your hour of anxiety," Wheeler wrote in the May 12, 1944, letter.

On May 17, 1944, Butte's newspaper, the *Montana Standard*, reported that 1st Lt. Robert Muri was among six Montanans, and 890 soldiers altogether, being held as prisoners of war. The Germans held him and other captured Allied airmen in Stalag Luft 1, a prison camp near Barth, Western Pomerania, Germany.

It's said that the Allies, aware of the prison camp, avoided Barth in their bombing runs. About 9,000 airmen — 7,588 American and 1,351 British and Canadian — were imprisoned at Luft 1 when Russian troops liberated them on the night of April 30, 1945.

Robert spent almost 15 months in the POW camp; word of his liberation took more than a month to reach Montana. He was among 15 Montana airmen freed after the fall of German, the *Billings Gazette* said on June 12, 1945. Others liberated hailed from all corners of the Treasure State: Missoula, Terry, Forest Grove, Kalispell, Butte, Antelope, Paradise, Great Falls, Ronan, Pompeys Pillar and Neihart.

Although Jim was no longer flying combat missions from the fall of 1942 on, being in a command role at Eglin wasn't a cushy, stateside posting. Officers in the Army and all branches of the armed service led — and still lead — the fliers, soldiers and sailors in their ranks in honoring fallen comrades at military funerals. Those funerals, often coming after fatal plane crashes, happened at Eglin while Jim was there, and he may have been involved in having deceased fliers sent elsewhere in the U.S. for burial.

Jim got an immediate reminder of flyer mortality away from battle when he arrived at Eglin and became commander of the torpedo training program in October 1942. Muri's quick increase in responsibility followed the non-combat death of his predecessor, Lt. Col. George E. Pierce, who died in a plane crash on October 19, 1942. (Field Two at the current Eglin Air Force Base is named for Pierce.)

An incomplete list of fatal plane crashes at or near Eglin, or involving Army Air Force pilots based at Eglin who crashed on missions elsewhere, during Jim's stint as commander follows. Newspaper articles didn't usually mention the model of planes flown in mishaps, but it's safe to assume that some of them involved the planes Jim worked with, B-26 and B-25 medium bombers, as he trained pilots and crews in torpedo tactics. Army airmen would have tried to take time to pay respects to fallen fellow fliers irrespective of what planes they flew, or which branch of the military they were part of. Examples of the frequent tragedy that was part of war include:

- August 1943, when the crash of an Army medium bomber killed six men on a routine training flight. The bomber, based at Barksdale Field in Louisiana, crashed into the Gulf of Mexico near Eglin. Observers saw the plane hit the water, burst into flames and sink. Responders to the crash found no trace of survivors, according to the *Panama City* (FL) *News-Herald* (August 12, 1943).

- December 1942, when three occupants of an Army plane died when the aircraft, making a cross-country flight, crashed between the Florida cities of Pensacola and Crestview (*Tampa, FL, Tribune*, December 2, 1942).

- A pair of mountain crashes three weeks apart, in December 1943 and January 1944. In the first crash, two men in a light bombing plane died when it crashed into the side of a Tennessee mountain. The plane's home base was Eglin, so its commanding officer notified relatives of the deaths, according to the *Pensacola News Journal* (December 31, 1943). Soon after came the crash of A-78 Army plane into a mountain in Virginia, killing the pilot and the enlisted man with him, according to the *News Journal* (January 22, 1944). Based at Eglin, the men were flying to Bolling Field in Washington, D.C.

- The Navy had a major presence in the Pensacola area, and several of its planes crashed with fatalities. One mid-air collision cost the lives of four Pensacola Air Training Center fliers, said the *News Journal* (August 14, 1943).

It wasn't all gloom, however, for the Army aviators at Eglin. In late 1943, Brig. Gen. Grandison Gardner, Eglin's commander, received the Army Air Force's distinguished service award for safety. The honor reflected a sharp drop in the rate of Army aircraft training accidents during fiscal year 1943 compared with the previous years, the *News Journal* reported on November 14, 1943.

Gardner said the accident rate fell in a year when flight hours increased 190 percent from the year before. However, he said, Army pilots would fly many more hours in faster and larger planes. Therefore, he called for "even greater efforts to protect our flying personnel and to keep our accident rate down."

Jim took flying seriously, but as a battle-seasoned pilot, he didn't shy away from occasional levity in the cockpit. His son, James, tells a story he heard that bears out that side of his father's personality.

One day, Jim took a general up for a check ride in a B-26; a check ride makes up the final examination to get or maintain certification as a pilot. Jim turned the plane over to the general, who flew for a while.

"OK, take it back down as fast as you can," the general said, yielding the controls to Jim, who began a falling leaf, an aerobatic maneuver in which a plane goes into a wings-level stall — it stops flying and falls. The pilot uses the rudder to counter the spin, which begins a spin in the opposite direction. The pilot repeats the process as often as desired, and throughout, the plane resembles a leaf falling from the sky, slipping to one side, stopping and then slipping in the other direction.

That trick distressed the general so much he threw up.

Chapter 15 – A B-26 flight with Jimmy Doolittle?

Did Jim Muri, as pilot, and Jimmy Doolittle, as his co-pilot, fly together in a B-26 after taking off from Eglin Field (or at another Florida base) during World War II? Jim's family members have long believed so, and his so-far-undisputed recollection of that event appears in two accessible accounts — the archives of the B-26 Marauder Historical Society, which contain the transcript of a 1990 interview where Muri recalled his flight with Doolittle, and an article in the *Billings Gazette*, in which Muri also discussed the flight with reporter Tom Howard.

Those published reports make a strong case for answering "yes" to whether Muri spent a few hours together in the cockpit of a B-26 with perhaps the most famed pilot of World War II.

The problem lies in saying when or where a Muri-Doolittle flight occurred. No documentation pinpointing a date or location is available. But based on the historical record, it is possible to construct one scenario for the event, which says the flight may have occurred in February or March 1944.

The B-26, known as a "hot" plane that required a skilled pilot at the controls to avoid a crackup, compiled a high crash rate during training flights in 1942 and 1943. Doolittle traveled to bases throughout the U.S. and in North Africa and took AAF pilots along on demonstration flights to prove the B-26's airworthiness. Those flights could have included one in 1944 with Muri at Eglin.

Decades later, the details remain fuzzy, but Muri related flying with Doolittle twice to interviewers, in 1990 when he was in his early 70s and again in 2003 as he neared his 85th birthday. Neither account has been disproven.

In the summer of 1990, Jim and Alice Muri got a visit at their Reedpoint, Montana, home, where they had retired two decades earlier, from a representative of the B-26 Marauder Historical Society. Dick Ellinger, the visitor, traveled to the Treasure State from the group's headquarters at the time, Ashland, Ohio; the society is now based in Tucson, Arizona.

Ellinger conducted a videotaped interview, which Ellen Oyster, a society board member and the group's senior archivist, transcribed. She mailed a copy of the transcript to Jim in September 1991; the transcript contains Jim's account of a visit by Doolittle to Eglin Field in Florida, the base where Muri served as commander of the torpedo training school from October 1942 until April 1944.

Jim told Ellinger that most of his Marauder experience was "with the old clipped-wing B-26, the old one, which was the fast one, the real original." He did, however, fly later models of the B-26, and Jim said he flew an updated B-26 with the man who led 16 B-25 bombers off the deck of the carrier Hornet in the April 1942 raid on Tokyo.

"I had the occasion of flying the B-26F with Jimmy Doolittle when the Martin Company was trying to save the production toward the end of the war.

"They sent Jimmy Doolittle around in an F-model airplane to demonstrate this particular airplane, and the difference between it and the regular B-26s was the warped wing. When you flew the 'F'' straight and level, the nose was down because the wing had been warped, and it brought the nose down in cruise."

Jim said he flew a B-26 for several hours one day with Doolittle as his co-pilot. The two "climbed out on one engine, flew around, feathered the good engine, and came around, in a fully loaded condition, and landed at Eglin Field."

"Then we'd taxi back and take off, and after we got off the ground, he would reach over and feather it, and we would climb out again," Jim said.

Those brief flights continued a whole afternoon, "demonstrating to the powers that be that this was a safe flying airplane," he said.

He repeated the story in October 2003, after he received word that the World War II Veterans Committee had awarded him the Jimmy Doolittle Award for outstanding services to the Air Corps. The committee invited him to come to Washington, D.C., to receive the award, which he did, as reported by the *Billings Gazette* (October 8, 2003).

In the article, Jim told Howard about his time in the cockpit of a B-26 with Jimmy Doolittle during World War II.

After the bomber took off, it lost power in the right engine. Unbeknownst to Jim, Doolittle had feathered the engine's propeller. Jim acted fast, righted the plane and realized what Doolittle was doing.

"He was proving to me that the airplane was completely safe," Jim said.

"Of course, he didn't have to. This was part of the school that I was to give the other pilots."

Despite its reputation as a tricky machine, the B-26 gained a lifetime loyalist in Muri, who believed it was the best American bomber of World War II — and that was something he had a frame of reference for because his two younger brothers flew heavy, four-engine bombers in the war. As mentioned earlier, Robert flew B-17s from England, and Andy piloted a B-24 Liberator in the Pacific.

The B-26 "was fast, tough and had a long range," Jim said.

He remembered Doolittle, who died in 1993 at age 96, as "magnificent. He was a small guy but very cool. He could fly anything."

As for the B-26F that he remembered flying one afternoon at Eglin with Doolittle, Jim said, "It was, of all the models, the best, simply because the airplane flew better with the nose in a down position. But the war being as far along as it was, they never did go into production on it to any great extent."

William Wolf's definitive volume on the B-26 includes a chapter about the F model. The Glen Martin Co. built 100 of these bombers, which started leaving the Baltimore factory in late February 1944. As Jim noted, the B-26F's "twisted wing" differentiated it from earlier Martin Marauders.

That modification produced several effects: a takeoff run shortened by about 300 feet from what was the standard before; a takeoff speed reduced to about 110 mph; and a landing run shorter by about 25 percent compared with the F's predecessors.

"During flight, the wing modifications gave the (B-26F) a slight tails up altitude, decreasing drag and slightly reducing the top speed of the Marauders to 277 mph," according to Wolf.

Pilot feedback mentioned that this Marauder did not handle as well as earlier models. The change in their wing arrangement meant Model Fs could carry 20 more gallons of gasoline, "but this extra fuel made little practical difference to combat range because of the increased drag generated by the new wing design," Wolf wrote.

Meanwhile, by early 1944, Doolittle was in transition from commanding the 12th Air Force in North Africa to his new role as commander of the Army's 8th Air Force, based in England. Planning for Operation Overlord, the invasion of Nazi-occupied France, was underway. It would culminate in the landing of Allied troops on the beaches of Normandy, an operation headed by Supreme Commander Dwight Eisenhower.

Doolittle's flight log shows him carrying out final duties in North Africa in early January 1944; that had been his primary base since late fall 1942. The rest of his flight log for January 1944, plus the logs for February, March and April of that year place him at bases in England.

Yet there are gaps in the logs, periods with no reported missions; these time frames are long enough to have made it possible for Doolittle to have flown to the U.S. He might have gone to AAF headquarters in Washington to confer with his boss, Air Force Chief Arnold. And what was to have prevented Doolittle from traveling to nearby Baltimore, stopping in at the Martin factory and checking out with a B-26-F for a flight to Florida? Where he might have dropped in at Eglin to look up Muri, one of the Air Force's most acclaimed B-26 pilots after *Susie-Q's* torpedo run in the Battle of Midway.

The most likely windows for a Muri-Doolittle flight at Eglin in 1944 include: January 11-24; January 27-February 14; and March 7-20. Doolittle's log shows no missions from April 6-14, 1944, and he would have been involved in final preparations for Operation Overlord by that time. It seems unlikely he would have had time in April 1944 for a flight to the U.S. and a test of the newest B-26.

By April 1944, Muri had received word that the Eglin torpedo training school would be shut down, and he may have already received orders for his next assignment as commander of the Watertown, South Dakota, air field. He and Alice could have been preparing to move with their one-year-old son, James, to their next military home about 2,000 miles north of the Florida Panhandle.

Something else could have drawn Doolittle to Eglin in the early months of 1944: curiosity about or even providing technical help to a movie that was being filmed there about a legendary mission he led in the Pacific. Ted Lawson, pilot of one of 16 B-25s that took off from the USS Hornet in April 1942, later co-authored an eyewitness account of the daring Tokyo Raid.

"Thirty Seconds Over Tokyo," by Lawson and Robert Considine, was published in 1943. Helped perhaps by Lawson's Hollywood connections as a Southern California native, the best-seller garnered him a contract for screen rights with MGM.

By February 1944, crews from MGM were on location at Eglin, filming the movie, according to the Pensacola News Journal (February 7, 1944). Eglin was an obvious setting for much of the opening footage because that was where pilots and crews of the Army Air Force's 17th Group, 95th Squadron — Lawson and his crew among them — trained for the raid. Assisted by a Navy officer with carrier expertise, Army pilots practiced taking off on short runways, several hundred feet long, a simulation of what they would experience taking off from the Hornet. The takeoff limits on the Eglin runways were marked with paint, but Doolittle kept details of the mission secret from the Army airmen until they and their B-26s had boarded the carrier and were sailing away from San Francisco Bay.

In one of the ironies that abound in World War II, and all

modern wars, it's possible there was a connection between Muri and Doolittle even before they flew a B-26 together. Jim arrived at Eglin in late September 1942 and soon became commander of the torpedo training school. He and his students flew both B-26s and B-25s on flights over land and over the Gulf of Mexico. It's possible they took off from the same runways used earlier by the Doolittle Raiders.

In 2019, the question remains unanswered: Did Jim Muri fly with Jimmy Doolittle at Eglin Field during World War II? The answer may never be known, even after one consults flight logs for both men, because of gaps in record-keeping during the war and because it's likely all who might have witnessed the flight and verified its participants are now dead.

One of the most knowledgeable individuals about the B-26, retired Navy officer Marshall Magruder, a son of the plane's chief designer, Peyton Magruder, maintains a voluminous library of books and other material about the B-26 in his home. He has researched the Marauder and its pilots for years. He says he cannot confirm Jim's account of a flight with Doolittle.

In a March 2018 email message, Marshall Magruder noted that Doolittle took command of the 12th Air Force in September 1942. That unit was preparing for the November 1942 landings in North Africa, a prelude to the Casablanca Conference of January 1943, where President Franklin Roosevelt and British Prime Minister Winston Churchill planned Allied strategy in Europe for the next phase of World War II.

After leading the air war in North Africa, Doolittle assumed command of the 15th Air Force, followed by command of the 8th Air Force from 1944 until V-E Day ended the war in Europe in

May 1945.

"To the best of the information that I have, (Doolittle) probably did not go to Eglin while in command of those North African and European Air Forces," Magruder said.

After seeing the Marauder Society video interview of Muri and reading the transcript, Magruder pointed out that Muri referenced Arnold and Army Chief of Staff General George Marshall as participants in torpedo training exercises at Eglin. Magruder said his research shows no Doolittle visits to Eglin after he trained B-25 pilots in simulated aircraft carrier there before they flew to San Francisco and boarded the *Hornet*, from which they launched the Tokyo raid.

Two of Jimmy Doolittle's living relatives, now adult grandchildren, said they had heard about their grandfather's efforts to save the B-26. But the elder Doolittle was a famed aviator who crossed paths with thousands of fellow fliers, worked with Arnold and received the Medal of Honor (for his leadership in the Tokyo Raid) from President Franklin Roosevelt in the White House.

Thus, the odds of Doolittle mentioning a specific Air Force pilot with whom he only had a brief interaction one afternoon — Jim Muri in this case — to his grandchildren are virtually nil. Jonna Doolittle Hoppes, a granddaughter, and her cousin Jimmy Doolittle III, a grandson, said in 2018 email messages they didn't know Muri as even a casual acquaintance of their grandfather.

So, take your pick: the account of the afternoon that Jim Muri flew together with Jimmy Doolittle in a B-26 in Florida, Muri as pilot and Doolittle as co-pilot, is a fine, fictional tale from a master storyteller — Muri — or something that happened.

In a March 2019 email, Hoppes said her grandfather's

autobiography shows "there is a good chance he flew with Muri. There just isn't any mention of who he actually flew with during these flights."

She said these incidents point to the possibility that Doolittle and Muri flew a B-26 together:

- Doolittle's visit to the Glenn Martin Co. factory in Baltimore and, soon thereafter, visits to several training bases and his efforts to "do his best" to save the B-26

- A separate mission to demonstrate the capabilities of the B-26 to pilots worried they would die flying it in a non-combat situation before they even got into battle.

In his autobiography, Doolittle discusses the first incident, which occurred at a time apparently early in World War II — he doesn't specify a year and month — when he and his wife, Josephine "Joe" Doolittle, became empty-nesters. Both of their sons had embarked on their own military careers. First-born Jimmy completed two years of college study in mechanical engineering and entered Army Air Force flight training. Younger son John received an appointment to the U.S. Military Academy and began his plebe (first) year at West Point.

Their parents moved into an apartment in Washington, D.C., and Jimmy Doolittle reported to Hap Arnold's office for an assignment that turned out to involve the B-26. Arnold assigned Doolittle to investigate the flight-worthiness of the Marauder, which had gained the unwanted reputation as a fast, unforgiving plane that killed pilots in training at an alarming rate.

"Hap asked me to check into the problem and recommend whether or not the B-26 should continue to be built," Doolittle

181

wrote. "I checked out in it at the Martin factory near Baltimore and liked it. There wasn't anything in its flying characteristics that good piloting skills couldn't overcome."

At about the same time, Doolittle said he traveled to several pilot training schools and B-26 units, met with student pilots and asked their opinions of the plane. Hearing all the perceived negatives of the Marauder, Doolittle then climbed into a B-26 and displayed various in-flight moves that were thought undoable. They included flying with one engine, turning into a dead engine and landing on one engine.

He completed the routines without a co-pilot, proving to doubters that pilots who paid close attention could survive, even excel at, "impossible" maneuvers in a B-26.

"I had no trouble getting volunteers after demonstrations," Doolittle said, providing no names of those who flew with him in B-26 demonstration flights other than Paul Leonard, his crew chief on the Tokyo raid; Clare Bunch; and Paul Tibbets, who later gained fame as the pilot of *Enola Gay*, which dropped the first atomic bomb in history on Hiroshima in August 1945.

The other episode apparently happened in the fall of 1942, perhaps before Doolittle went to North Africa to command Army Air Force units at the start of the Allied campaign against German and Italian forces.

"Those beginning weeks" were marred by a "very high rate of training accidents in the B-26 Marauder," Doolittle said.

"The word was out that it was a 'killer,' and I suspect that many crew members were convinced they could never survive the war in that airplane, not because of the enemy but because they would meet their maker in a non-combat accident."

Doolittle said he had tested the B-26 before many crews saw one, so it was his job to show them "it was a plane to be respected but not feared." Accompanied by Leonard as co-pilot, Doolittle visited "various B-26 units to show that it could easily be flown as a one-pilot airplane, although regulations required two pilots on every flight."

Doolittle's autobiography does not say which B-26 units he visited and when, and it thus leaves open the possibility he may have flown at bases, abroad and in the U.S., with pilots other than Leonard beside him in the cockpit.

Here is another theory: that Jimmy Doolittle and Jim Muri flew together in a B-26, in Florida, in mid-October 1942, just before Doolittle headed to his new command in North Africa.

Backing for this scenario comes from a historical novel, "Widow Maker: A Novel of World War II," a fact-based story centered on the B-26 and those who flew it, written by E.R. Johnson. Johnson portrays a meeting between Doolittle and Hap Arnold on October 17, 1942, in Arnold's office at USAAF headquarters in Washington.

Doolittle was ready to go overseas and take part in Operation Torch, the invasion of North Africa, but Arnold had a task he wanted Doolittle to complete before he left.

That year, more than 200 pilots had been killed in training accidents while flying B-26s. No wonder the Truman Committee wanted to cancel the government's contract with the Glenn Martin Co. and shut down B-26 production.

Arnold was emphatic in his instructions to Doolittle.

"I want you to go down to McDill Field in person and find out what's wrong with that airplane. Find out why it's killing so many of my pilots."

Arnold gave Doolittle his assignment: fly to McDill, put the B-26 through its paces and report back to the Air Force Chief of Staff. Doolittle had one week to carry out the project.

One week later, Doolittle was back in Arnold's office. He told his superior officer there was nothing mechanically wrong with the B-26 and that above all, better pilot training plus improved maintenance procedures would make it a reliable bomber. Doolittle said he took Captain Vince Burnett with him on the McDill mission, and they gave the B-26 a full flight evaluation.

Burnett stayed behind at McDill to rewrite the B-26 training manual, retrain instructor pilots and oversee changes in operational training. Doolittle was confident these reforms would transform the B-26's tarnished image into that of an airplane that could perform a vital role in the U.S. war effort.

It's plausible that Jim Muri, who had just arrived at Eglin in late September 1942, and Jimmy Doolittle, preparing to leave for North Africa but still in the states in mid-October 1942, could have crossed paths at a Florida air base. Whether it was at McDill or Eglin, several hours' flying time away, remains an open question.

One trouble spot in this hypothesis is Muri's specific reference in his B-26 Marauder Historical Society interview to having taken the F model of the plane up in the air. The F was still 16 months away from production in October 1942. Perhaps Jim got confused about the specific version of the B-26 that he flew with Jimmy Doolittle on that fateful day. We may never know.

Chapter 16 – Saving the Beloved B-26

Jim's recollection of his time at Eglin describes his frequent contact with top Army brass while he was there.

Early in the war, General Harold "Hap" Arnold was a proponent of torpedo bombing, having seen its effectiveness when used by Japanese planes against British warships in Asia. That led Arnold to issue orders that Army Air Force fliers, the B-26 men in particular, work with the Navy to develop better torpedo techniques.

When Jim got to Elgin, he reported to Brig. Gen. Barney Giles, then assistant to Arnold. Between Muri and Giles in the chain of command was a "retired Navy Chief who was then a lieutenant colonel in the (Army) named George Younkin. Now, George was a Navy man at heart. He was a believer in torpedoes, and he was a complete success when it came to coordinating between my organization at Eglin Field and General Giles, thence to General Arnold."

Jim said he had access to the highest ranks of Army brass while at Eglin. He could contact his superiors and ask for Arnold's help — with the possibility that General Marshall, the Army Chief of Staff, would be briefed on the matter.

If there was trouble, "he (Arnold) personally would come down and watch the demonstration we put on — go out on the target boats — yes, any number of times General Arnold was down there.

"He convinced General Marshall to come down one time (and) sit out on that target boat, watching those B-26s come in [and dropping] those torpedoes. Enough to scare anybody to death unless they knew it was air in there instead of tarpex that was the explosive at the time."

Jim's daughter, Sylvia, also has found evidence of at least a casual link between her mother, Alice, and Arnold's wife when her parents were at Eglin. "I found a card for Mom as a member of the National Association of Air Forces Women signed by Mrs. Henry H. Arnold, President," Sylvia said in a February 27, 2019, text message.

Late in World War II, with Allied victory almost certain, famed reporter Ernie Pyle gave the B-26 his stamp of approval.

Just before American troops hit the beaches at Normandy in June 1944, Pyle flew with a Marauder squadron from a bomber station in England. His report began: "These are some of the boys who have been blasting out our invasion path on the continent of Europe. For nearly a year they have been hammering at the wall of defense the Germans have thrown up. How well they have blasted we will know before the summer is over."

"They are a squadron of B-26 Marauder bombers. They are representative of the entire mighty weight of the tactical bombers of the Ninth Air Force. I have come to spend a few days with them because I wanted to get a taste of the pre-invasion assault from the air standpoint before we get a mouthful of the invasion proper from the ground."

Pyle's syndicated column appeared in dozens of newspaper across the country and also in Montana newspapers, including the *Fallon County* (MT) *Times* (June 1, 1944) in the southeastern Treasure State town of Baker. It's possible that someone who knew the Muri family in nearby Rosebud and Custer counties noticed the June 1, 1944, piece, clipped it and mailed it to Jim's parents, R.P. and Nellie Muri, at the ranch in Carterville, or to Jim's widowed grandmother, Mary Johnson, living in Miles City.

By that time, Jim's assignment as commander of the B-26 torpedo training school at Eglin Field had ended. Still, it would have put a smile on the faces of Muri family members to read that Pyle had given his blessing to a line of twin-engine bombers, among them the famous *Susie-Q*, No. 1391, that their son and grandson had flown in the Midway maelstrom.

Pyle took off before dawn with a B-26 crew that included a pair of bombardiers, boys as he called them, from San Francisco and East St. Louis, Ill. The commander of the squadron hailed from Chico, Texas; he was a 25-year-old who in five years had advanced from enlisted man to the rank of colonel in charge of several thousand men.

Pyle described the B-26 as a "very fast" plane that carried two tons of bombs. He noted its early reputation as a "hot plane" that required pilots to have great skill to avoid adding themselves and their crews to the rolls of training-flight casualties.

"But the B-26 has lived down the bad name," Pyle reported. Men in the squadron he observed displayed strong loyalty to the Marauder, which they believed was better than any other military bomber. Here's why: "They like it because it can take quick and evasive action when the flak is bothersome, and because it can run pretty well from defenders." The B-26 record in Europe showed high bombing accuracy and a low accident rate — accidents were rare when other American warplanes still claimed lives of men away from the firefights over Nazi-controlled territory at an alarming frequency.

Pyle said the B-26 he rode in carried a light load so takeoff was quick. The engines made "a terrific chatter," but soon the bomber climbed to 12,000 feet. His plane and the rest of the squadron flew higher, turned and headed for an unspecified target. It wasn't a mission over enemy territory, so there was no danger of being shot down that day.

Pyle sat in the nose of the B-26, the plexiglass quarters occupied by the bombardier. There, he viewed what was below and around the plane.

"I squeezed into the tiny compartment," which barely had room for two men. The nook at the plane's nose blocked much of the engine's noise, leaving Pyle with a "clear and spectacular" panorama as daylight broke. He stayed in the nose until the Marauder was homeward bound and then moved to the co-pilot's seat.

"The sun came out, the air was smooth, and wonderful flying along there over England so early in the morning," Pyle concluded.

If Muri's family read this article, they might have remarked on the contrast between Pyle's flight and Jim's two years earlier at Midway. The Montana civilian "crew," as well as Jim's wife, Alice, if she read the article, might have said something to the effect that there was nothing peaceful about what Susie-Q's men put up with, all the Japanese planes shooting at them and ship anti-aircraft guns shelling the plane.

Jimmy Doolittle's affection for the B-26 led him to make it his personal plane for much of the Second World War.

The historical record also shows that Doolittle saved the B-26 from Congress' axe when the plane's tricky flying characteristics earned it a variety of unwelcome nicknames. They included

"Widowmaker," which referred to the wives left behind by pilots killed in flight accidents; "One a Day in Tampa Bay," a nod to the frequent B-26 crashes into the bay after takeoff from nearby McDill Field in the early days of the war; and the "Baltimore Whore," so called because the B-26's short wings figuratively gave it no visible means of support. There were other labels, too, none of them flattering.

The Army Air Force Air Safety Board launched an investigation of the Marauder in the early months of 1942. The so-called Truman Committee, headed by the then Missouri senator and later vice president and then president, Harry Truman, swung into action, too. Talk that the War Department would shut down Marauder manufacturing was in the air.

General Arnold, an advocate of the B-26, took action to give the plane a fair shake. He assigned Doolittle, back from China after the Tokyo raid, to help prove the bomber was worth keeping.

Doolittle took part in one of the highest profile demonstrations of the B-26's performance, which occurred on September 11, 1942, at Wright Field in Dayton, Ohio. He and Bunch, his co-pilot, flew a bomber that was not fully equipped — it had full wing tanks, but other fuel and bombs were missing, and the two pilots and a crew man were aboard, leaving the B-26 short its full seven-man complement by four individuals. Pilot, co-pilot and tail gunner armor was not installed, and the .50-caliber nose, waste and tunnel guns were left behind.

"So perhaps this aircraft was not truly representative of bombers flown in combat and training," according to Wolf's "B-26 Marauder."

After his demonstration flights — Wright was just one —

Doolittle sent a memo to the Director of Military Requirements in September 1942. It made four points:

• That the B-26 was more difficult to fly than other planes of the time.

• That the plane had been in service long enough — manufacture started in 1940 — that fatigue or "wear out" failures were inclined to happen.

• That the planes needed top-quality maintenance but weren't getting it because of the urgency of getting B-26 units into combat zones overseas.

• That training also suffered from not taking into account the unique characteristics and limitations of the plane, aggravated by the rush to get Marauders to the front line.

Doolittle concluded by recommending a "complete review of policy and practice … in order to stop these accidents and derive the maximum utility from this plane."

Then, in the summer of 1943, came a bombshell: the Truman Committee's report, which was critical of the B-26 and several other military planes. The committee, however, spared the Army's four-engine, heavy bombers from censure, saying the Boeing B-17 Flying Fortress and the Consolidated B-24 Liberator performed well in war. Also, the North American B-25 Mitchell, a twin-engine bomber, got praise as "a valuable plane," according to the *Baltimore Sun* (July 11, 1943).

As for the B-26, the committee said the Army would discontinue production, and the panel damned the plane with faint praise. First, it said the bomber "has many difficulties." Then it said, "It has high performance, both in speed and load-carrying capacity, and, according to most reports, is an exceptionally fine plane in the air."

But the tone of the committee's review turned critical again. The B-26 "is unsafe when operated by any pilots except those specially trained for its operation because of unusual difficulties in landing and takeoff." The Marauder had logged a higher accident rate than the B-25, the public was told.

"As a fighting airplane, most pilots who know it (the Marauder) like it, and improvements have been made on it." Still, problems with the B-26, and the high cost of production and maintenance, prompted the Army to plan a shutdown of manufacturing. Martin Co. facilities in Baltimore and Omaha would shift to producing other types of planes, according to the report.

In an interview conducted three weeks before his death on September 27, 1993, Doolittle summarized his save-the-B-26 tour.

"The Martin B-26 Marauder was a tricky plane to fly, and many guys had been killed in it; therefore, it developed a reputation. I took Sergeant Paul Leonard with me, and we traveled to the various B-26 bases and demonstrated the proper handling and ease with which the Marauder could be flown.

"After that, the trust factor among pilots rose considerably, and the men were not reluctant to fly in it," he said.

The interview provides no details about the timeline for Doolittle and Leonard's campaign and which bases it stopped at.

Jimmy Doolittle III, a retired Air Force officer, said he has read about the Martin Marauders' role in the Battle of Midway, including Muri's piloting of *Susie-Q* in the opening attack.

Most of the books he has read mention the four B-26s that tried to launch torpedoes against the Japanese carrier *Akagi*. He also knew of the efforts "our grandpa Gen. Jimmy Doolittle put into

191

debunking the bad press that the B-26s got early on," most of which happened before the younger Doolittle's birth in 1944.

"Simply put, the high wing loading, faster approach speeds than most fighters (sic) of the day, and high minimum control speeds put the airplane beyond the level of competency of most of the instructor pilots of the day," he said.

The B-26 compiled an excellent combat record and "outclassed everything of its time from the standpoint of toughness, getting crews to and especially back from the target to refuel, rearm and get back in the air to attack," the younger Doolittle said.

"Flown by properly trained pilots, I am sure the B-26 had no more bad habits than many high performance, multi-engine airplanes of its time."

Doolittle said he regretted not hearing more first-hand stories about his grandfather's effort to save the B-26. He said he spent considerable time with his grandfather, and they hunted and fished together, "but (I) never pressed him to tell stories about his wartime experiences as he did not press me to tell mine."

Chapter 17 - A Hero's Life isn't Always Easy

The war dragged on while Jim was at Eglin. D-Day, the landing of Allied troops on the beaches of Normandy to start the final thrust toward Berlin, bringing Hitler's defeat, lay ahead. B-26s played a pivotal role in softening German defenses for the amphibian attack by U.S. and British infantryman on June 6, 1944. Also ahead were hard battles in Europe, one of the most famous of which, the Battle of the Bulge, occurred in the winter of 1944-45. Historic U.S. victories in the Pacific at Midway and Guadalcanal put the Japanese on permanent defense from 1942 on, yet Tito's government refused to surrender until atomic bombs fell on Hiroshima and Nagasaki, leaving the island nation's militaristic rulers no choice but to accept defeat.

For the Muris — Jim, Alice and their infant son, James — 1944 was a year of transition. The Army Air Force ended its torpedo training program at Eglin in April that year, and Jim got orders to report to the air field in Watertown, S.D., and take over as base commander.

Watertown, a municipal airport, became a military facility on July 20, 1942, when authorities approved the field for a satellite bomber air base affiliated with the Sioux City, Iowa, Air Base. The federal government took control of the airport and constructed the air base. A second Air Force cold-weather bomber training base, linked to the Sioux Falls, South Dakota, Army air field, functioned at Watertown's field, which also incorporated the Air Proving Ground Command.

B-17 Flying Fortress and B-24 Liberator units received

advanced training at Watertown before being sent overseas. Units stationed at Watertown included the 702nd Bomb Squadron of the 445th Bomb Group.

Watertown offered recreational opportunities to servicemen, too. It's not known if Jim took part, but if he wanted to, he could have resumed an activity he enjoyed at Eglin: playing on a base basketball team. Soldiers at the air field and local high school teachers joined forces, formed a squad and scheduled five benefit games to raise money for an infantile paralysis prevention drive. Opponents included four independent teams from neighboring towns plus one high school, according to the *Sioux Falls* (SD) *Argus-News* (January 17, 1945)

A Montana farm and ranch boy like Muri felt at home amid the grain fields of eastern South Dakota. In the summer of 1945, soldiers from Watertown helped shock grain in the area, a situation caused by the wartime shortage of farm labor. Jim organized the volunteer effort, mentioned in the *Argus-News* (August 10, 1945).

On one occasion, he had sad duty as the top-ranking officer at Watertown. In July 1945, a 26-year-old corporal from Kansas stationed at the base drowned in Lake Kampeska, according to the *Rapid City* (SD) *Journal* (July 23, 1945). Two companions recovered the man's body, Jim said. Base officials returned the body to Preston, Kansas, where his widow and a seven-month-old daughter survived the soldier.

The Muris became a family of four at Watertown with the birth of their daughter, Sylvia, on March 1, 1945; housing on the base was in short supply, so they lived in homes in Watertown until Jim's discharge from the Army on March 9, 1946.

As base commander, Jim worked with pilots and crew members

of heavy bombers, the B-17 and the B-24, but his association with his beloved B-26 and Eglin wasn't over. In September 1945, a hurricane in Florida forced the Air Force to evacuate 25 planes from Eglin to Watertown as a precaution against storm damage, according to the *Deadwood* (SD) *Pioneer-Times* (September 18, 1945). It's unknown what types of planes the Army sent to South Dakota, but given Eglin's use for B-26 training flights, odds are that the group included Martin Marauders.

Fifty-six years before 9/11, an airplane crashed into the side of the world's tallest skyscraper, and Jim played a minor role in the non-terrorist tragedy as a South Dakota base commander.

A B-25 checked out from Watertown slammed into the 79th floor of the Empire State Building in New York City on July 28, 1945. The crash led to the largest airship-related loss of life in the metropolitan area since the Hindenburg, a massive German dirigible, caught fire and was destroyed during its attempt to dock with its mooring mast at Naval Air Station Lakehurst on May 6, 1937, killing 36 people. The Empire State Building, impact point of the crash less than a decade later, was built in 1931 and stands 102 stories tall; with its antenna, it rises 1,454 feet. The building held the world's-tallest title until completion of the World Trade Center's North Tower in 1970.

Lt. Col. William F. Smith flew the twin-engine Mitchell that hit the building at 9:52 on a Saturday morning. A day-after article in the *Austin* (TX) *Sunday American-Statesman* (July 29, 1945) said the pilot was among at least 13 people killed in the accident. The crash injured another 20 individuals, according to the preliminary report.

V-E Day, May 7, 1945, ended the war in Europe, but Japan had not surrendered when the accident happened. Conflict in the

195

Pacific raged on until atomic bombs fell on Hiroshima and Nagasaki in early August 1945, prompting Emperor Hirohito to make an unprecedented radio address to his people, declaring the nation's fight with the U.S. and Great Britain was over. V-J Day — August 14, 1945 — ended the war.

Smith and crew member Staff Sergeant Christopher S. Domitrovich were scheduled to leave for combat in the Pacific before the crash. They took off from Pierre, S.D., in the B-25 that lit up the skies over New York. Military planes came through South Dakota, which was a stopover place en route to other destinations.

It wasn't unusual that Jim, as commander of the Watertown base and then a major outranked by Smith, gave him permission to use the B-25 from Watertown's fleet, Sylvia Saadati said in a March 2019 telephone conversation. Thus, a cross-country flight from South Dakota that ended in destruction and death started with one AAF pilot understanding the needs of another to get flight time.

Smith left from the field at nearby Sioux Falls, S.D., according to the *Arizona Republic* of Phoenix (August 1, 1945). He had 1,000 hours of combat flight time but was making the flight to Newark, N.J., to keep his status as a pilot entitled to flight pay, the Army said later.

The Army required Air Force pilots to fly a specified number of hours each month to qualify for flight pay, and Smith would have received six hours credit for the flight.

He flew to Bedford, Mass., and delivered three passengers there before turning around for the return flight.

The *New York Times* revisited the tragedy for a July 28, 1970, story. The article said Smith, a decorated veteran of 34 missions in

Europe, was gaining cross-country experience before his expected redeployment in the Pacific.

Smith was flying from Bedford to Newark and traveling at about 200 miles per hour when he got lost in the mist and steered his plane into the skyscraper at the 79th floor, 913 feet above the street.

Air controllers advised Smith to land at New York Municipal Airport-LaGuardia Field, now LaGuardia Airport, but he asked for the weather at Newark. The War Department — now the Defense Department — investigated and concluded that the pilot "erred in judgment when he elected to fly over Manhattan in weather conditions which prevailed at the time," and controllers should not have cleared him to land at Newark.

The *Times* said civil air regulations at the time required all planes to fly at least 2,000 feet above Manhattan — more than 1,000 feet higher than Smith's altitude when he crashed.

When the B-25 hit the building, the plane's gasoline tanks exploded. Orange flames erupted and rose to the 86th-floor observatory. The impact sheared off the bomber's wings, and one engine and part of the landing gear plummeted down an elevator shaft into a subbasement. The other engine careened across the 78th floor, punched through the south wall and fell on the roof of a building on 33rd Street.

Only a skeleton staff of the organization headquartered at the crash point of impact, the War Relief Services of the National Catholic Welfare Conference on the 79th floor, was at work that day.

One survivor, Catherine O'Connor, then secretary to the relief agency's executive director, described her perspective on the tragedy a quarter-century later. O'Connor had been reading the morning mail and walking across her office when she heard "a terrific explosion … and then the building rocking so," she told the *Times*.

A "burst of flames which consumed the office instantaneously" as flaming gasoline hit the building, came next.

"We had no idea what happened," O'Connor said, so she and coworkers ran for shelter in a room on the skyscraper's 33rd Street side. They waited, "completely surrounded by flames and in pitch-black smoke."

"Believe it or not, we prayed," she said. "We knew this was the end, we knew there was no way out. … You had strange thoughts, thoughts of many things, and prayed."

It took at least an hour before firefighters could remove O'Connor and her companions from their fiery sanctuary. Doctors treated her for burned feet, caused by the heat of the floors, and shock, and she never fully recovered from the smoke poisoning she suffered that day.

By 1970, the official death toll had been finalized at 14, including Smith, Domitrovich and a Navy machinist's mate who had hitched a ride on the B-25 so he could go home and see his parents in Brooklyn. The other fatalities, and most of the 26 injured, came from the relief agency's staff.

No record of Jim's reaction to news of the crash exist. He had to take the tragedy in stride. Stoicism in the face of daily death was part of the makeup of American soldiers, sailors and fliers in World War II.

Describing her father in 2019, six years after his death, Sylvia Saadati said, "The raconteur was very stoic when he hurt. He could not have felt responsible for the man who had flown so many missions having made an uninformed decision that results in disaster.

"But it hurts when one of your own is lost."

On March 9, 1946, Muri's time in the Army Air Force, a run of 10 years, ended. World War II was over, and the military discharged many officers as part of its downsizing. However, talk of change that could allow someone like Muri to continue his military career was in the air. Congress was pondering the concept of a unified defense department, which would end the War Department and bring the Army and Navy under the purview of a single cabinet secretary.

And where would military planes and personnel end up? The Navy prevailed in its argument that air war at sea was best waged with planes that took off from carriers. As for air war launched from land, that became the domain of a new separate U.S. Air Force within the Department of Defense.

As the machinations in Washington, D.C., continued, Jim Muri needed to provide for a family of four while he waited for his hoped-for commission in the Air Force. He needed a job, so he worked for a dealer that sold farm equipment manufactured by International Harvester and checked the mail for authorization that would allow a seasoned 27-year-old military pilot to continue flying.

In a 2019 phone conversation, Sylvia shared one memory of her family's time at Watertown, passed down to her because she was too young then to have remembered. The Muris had moved to a house that sat on the shore of a lake in the Watertown area. On one of Alice's trips back to stay with her mother in Riverside while

Jim tried to find housing for his family, she brought back Anne Moyer's dog, a collie named Thor. The animal assumed the duty of helping keep his infant charges safe — he would take turns laying on Jim and Sylvia so they wouldn't wander into the water.

On June 5, 1947, Jim got the telegram he was waiting for. He read it and said to Alice, "Honey, the Air Force wants me to report to Great Falls." An opportunity to resume his military career required that he go to an airfield the Army built near the north-central Montana city early in World War II. The field served during the war as the southern end of an air route that connected to Ladd Field in Fairbanks, Alaska, which was used for the U.S. Lend-Lease program that supplied the Soviet Union with aircraft and supplies to fight the German Army.

Jim's destination was then called the Great Falls Army Air Base. The Air Force renamed the facility as Malmstrom Air Force Base in 1955, and it keeps strategic importance today as one of three Air Force bases that maintain and operate the Minuteman III intercontinental ballistic missile.

The telegram said Jim needed to report in 15 days for a physical exam if he were still interested in joining the Army Air Force, which was in transition then. The Department of Defense, created on September 18, 1947, replaced the War Department and brought the Army, Navy, Marine Corps and the newly established Air Force together under unified command.

Jim's permanent commission in the peacetime army came through just before that, in May 1947, when President Truman submitted a list of about 9,200 officers of the army, reserve corps and national guard for Senate confirmation. Evidently, Jim was among forty-six Montanans who made the list, reported by the

Great Falls Tribune (May 31, 1947).

The Army used a selective process to choose peacetime officers, picking about 13 percent of the 70,000 candidates nationwide with wartime service. That May 1947 list was part of the second phase of a program to integrate officers into non-combat roles. In 1946, 10,800 individuals made the cut, and the Pentagon offered commissions to about 1,850 Army officers in 1947. The Army announced further nominees that summer.

Alice Muri and her toddlers – Jimmy, as young James was called until he outgrew that name in the early 1950s, and Sylvia – went to R.P. and Nellie Muri's ranch in Carterville while Jim headed several hundred miles north in Montana to his next post.

Jim, a major when he left the Army in 1946, kept that rank at the Great Falls Army Air Base, where he became executive officer of the 24th transport squadron, according to the *Tribune* (October 18, 1947).

When Jim arrived in Montana's "Electric City," so named because of hydroelectric dams on each of the five cascades of the Great Falls of the Missouri River, the city was experiencing a post-war boom. Great Falls was on the verge of surpassing Butte to become Montana's most populous city. That happened in 1950, when the census counted 39,214 people in Great Falls.

The Great Falls Army Air Base's crucial role in World War II is well-known. In fact, it's a key element in one book by the Treasure State's best-known modern novelist, Ivan Doig. In "The Eleventh Man," Doig depicts Women Air Service Pilots, WASPs, ferrying P-39 fighter planes from Great Falls to Alaska, where other pilots took the controls and flew them to the Soviet Union as part of the Lend Lease program.

Tribune readers got their first insight into the base's workings in an August 28, 1944, article. Previously restricted in what it could report because of the need for wartime secrecy and with Nazi defeat now seeming to be imminent, the city's newspaper recounted the base's evolution from a heavy-bomber training unit in May 1942 to the point, starting in 1943, when the base functioned as part of the AAF's Air Transport Command, Alaska division.

Its new duty turned the base into a "gateway for an aerial delivery route for planes being sent from this nation to Russia ..."

"Because of its situation on the route to Russia through Canada and Alaska, bombers, P-39s, rubber seed and all matter imaginable to help stem Germany's military might, has gone through East base (part of the Great Falls base)," the *Tribune* said.

Jim reported to the Great Falls base while residents were still reeling from the tragedy that took place in the sky over their city 10 months earlier, which many had witnessed. Because the accident involved Army Air Force bombers that had taken off from the Great Falls base and because it triggered an official investigation, Jim undoubtedly knew of the mid-air collision that killed six people, injured 25 more and also caused the death of 25 race horses in a fairgrounds barn.

The disaster occurred during the day's featured event of the Northern Montana State Fair — now the Montana State Fair — on August 9, 1946. An air show pulled in a crowd, but the fair's expected highlight turned into what the *Tribune* (August 10, 1946) called the greatest disaster in the history of Montana fairs. Now, 73 years later, the accident probably still holds that distinction.

By 1946, the Army was phasing out the B-26 in favor of another bomber often mentioned interchangeably with the Marauder, the Douglas A-26 Invader. They were different planes. Production of the A-26, also a twin-engine aircraft, began in September 1943, just as B-26 production was peaking. The A-26 could fly 100 mph faster than the B-26 with a heavier bomb load. As few as two people could fly an A-26, the pilot operating a nose gun and a crewman doubling as navigator and bombardier, although on most missions, a third crew member operated the rear guns. In comparison, a standard B-26 complement included seven people — the pilot, co-pilot and five crewmen.

In the first minutes of the air show, two Army A-26 Invaders collided overhead, horrifying more than 20,000 spectators in the grandstands. Two of the three bombers smashed into each other after coming into view of the crowd. The planes became tangled and spewed wreckage into the infield as they swept by the grandstands at almost 400 mph. Here's what happened, as reported by the *Tribune* :

"The lead plane, its tail sheared, crashed at the north end of the race track, plunged into a horse barn and hurtled across the grounds more than 900 feet, leaving a mass of burning debris. The second plane, its wing destroyed, veered dizzily out of view and crashed in the hills five miles north of the fairgrounds. The third plane, its tail damaged, returned safely to the east base to make a crash landing."

Besides the four Army fliers, victims included a young college student, the 17-year-old daughter of an East Base employee, and a 36-year-old stableman, both in the barn when the A-26 struck.

Gen. Carl Spaatz, commander of the AAF, ordered an investigation of the crash, according to the *Tribune* (August 10,

1946). An Army statement said the planes were flying about 390 mph at a safe altitude of about 500 feet when the crash occurred.

Things happened quickly as 1947 went on. "The house (in Great Falls) is signed and sealed, and you'll love it," Jim said in an October 2 letter to his wife. "Bring Thor with you, and send for our stuff still in Riverside."

Jim became part of base life long enough to chair the Great Falls' air field's campaign for the local Community Chest drive in late October 1947, according to the *Tribune* (October 22, 1947).

Alice barely had time to get herself and the children settled, first in Cartersville and then in Riverside, when the Air Force threw the Muris another curveball. On January 10, 1948, Jim wrote from Japan. The Army assigned him to the Occupation Army for postwar observation, outreach and oversight duty on the outskirts of Tokyo.

Those rapid-fire changes in her officer husband's life wore on Alice. "Mom had to have hated that quick transition. She just wanted to be together as a family," her daughter said.

Jim lived in Japan for about six months before he could bring his family over. Alice and the children stayed at Grandma Anne Moyer's house on Hillcrest in Riverside, where Sylvia remembers playing with a cousin much of the time.

"Dad was being trained for that Japan mission. There was a lot he needed to get taught," Sylvia said.

Jim wrote another letter, telling Alice he had been named group executive and commanding officer of the headquarters squadron, one of five squadrons in his group. Jim's letter said he was very lonely and having trouble making friends, something not helped by his rank. He was a major, and most officers at the base were lieutenants wary of friendship with higher-ranking officers.

Also, other officers spent many nights getting drunk, but Jim preferred drinking two beers at most in the evening. Squadron dynamics displeased the general in charge, he said.

Jim shared one pleasant piece of news: he would referee a basketball game. He omitted whether he, as a 29-year-old former prep star in Montana, got to lace up sneakers, but at least he was around a sport he loved.

When all four Muris got to live together abroad, they took up residence in military housing in the Grant Heights Section of Camp Drake, one of 20 military installations in the Tokyo area. The camp was built for the Japanese army, and the U.S. used it during the post-war occupation of the country. Camp Drake was about 30 minutes by train from Tokyo.

Sylvia remembers living in one of several long, two-story houses joined together, possibly barracks converted to family quarters. Her family lived in a house that faced the street.

The house had a crawl space underneath, which occupants accessed through a trap door in a closet downstairs. The space provided a pleasant surprise for a young American girl one day.

"There's a cat meowing down there," said Sylvia, perhaps 3 then. She wanted a pet cat, so she opened the trap door and enticed the cat to come into her family's living area.

The Muris' time in Japan didn't lack trauma and drama.

"I was shot in the arm one month to the day after my 4th birthday," Sylvia said. "My brother shot me. I ended up in a military hospital getting penicillin."

A report filed with Camp Drake military police said a call about the incident came in at 4 p.m. on April 1, 1949.

"James Muri, age 5, accidentally shot his sister, Sylvia, age 4, in the left arm with a .45-caliber revolver while playing with the gun," the report said. MP headquarters dispatched an old fashioned military ambulance with side-mounted benches to the Muri residence at unit 358-D.

There, ambulance attendants found Sylvia standing at the second-floor railing, sobbing, with blood covering most of her small body.

"What happened?" one of the ambulance attendants asked people at the scene as they loaded a wailing Sylvia into the vehicle.

MPs got the story. The family's maids had put Jimmy and Sylvia down for their afternoon nap, but Jimmy got up. He said he was looking for the Easter basket he was sure his parents hid in their closet.

Awoken by her brother rustling about, Sylvia got up. She watched him get a higher-up view into the closet so he could see what was there.

That's how he found one of two revolvers lying on the shelf. He picked up one gun that had a shell in the chamber, but the boy didn't know that.

The Muris' two maids were busy in the kitchen while the children played upstairs.

"So, we snuck into my parents' room, which was five feet from ours, down the hall. We were going to go looking for hidden goodies. We were smart. We knew there was something. We could actually see the Easter bunny ears sticking up from the top closet shelf," Sylvia said.

Her brother used a trunk to climb up for a better look at the rabbit, but Jimmy came down with something else: a revolver from a set of Colt .45s his father got earlier in his military career, possibly while stationed in Hawaii, according to Sylvia.

"They were beautiful, long-barreled pistols. He had the holster to go with them."

Jimmy and Sylvia knew about but had no real interest in their father's pistols. When they played, they pretended to have Old West confrontations using Jimmy's toy guns made of plastic and wood.

"We started playing cowboys and Indians. He said, 'Stick 'em up.' Not that he meant to shoot. I don't think he even knew they were real," Sylvia said.

Tapping her "vivid memories" of the incident, she recalled wearing a two-piece bathing suit on a warm day.

Playing along with the mock holdup, "I put my hands up. Imagine how small a 4-year-old is. My hands are up in the air."

"What he didn't know is there was a hair trigger on the pistol."

The gun fired, sending a bird-shot shell loaded with BBs at Sylvia.

"It hit me on the underside of my left arm, on the side where my heart is, two inches away."

Hearing the gunshot, the maids hurried upstairs. They saw Sylvia standing on the landing, covered in blood, and almost fainted. Neighbor women came running with blankets. By the time the medics arrived, people had wrapped Sylvia in several blankets. No one opened them to assess her wound, but a medic asked a bystander where she was hurt.

In 2019, Sylvia recalled medics "throwing me into the bottom of a tin can," her term for the old fashioned ambulance. They asked bystanders where she was hurt, then took her to the base dispensary for first-aid treatment. The wound wasn't thought serious, but to err on the side of caution, those in charge decided she should to go to the 9th General Hospital.

"I remember being thrown to the bottom of that damned military ambulance, literally thrown on my hurt arm. They didn't know what was wrong with me. I don't think anybody knew where I was hurt," she said.

Told where Sylvia's mother's bridge party was, the ambulance driver stopped to pick up Alice.

"She ... sits on the bench, and I'm trying to tell her" where she was wounded, Sylvia said.

"I'm hysterical, I'm gulping air, and I'm crying. I'm trying to tell her I'm lying on my hurt arm, and nobody's listening to me."

The hospital placed Sylvia among bedridden patients in the children's ward. She could get up and walk around, so she shared candy that people brought for her with the other children.

A less-pleasant part of her brief hospital stay involved her dealings with military nurses used to war wounds who had little or no training in treating children. Her wound looked like hamburger, and they placed a huge gauze bandage over it. When attendants needed to change the dressing, they found the bandage glued to her skin by congealed blood.

A nurse applied hydrogen peroxide to make removing the bandage easier, but that made matters worse.

"I screamed bloody murder," Sylvia said.

Another nurse tried a bribe the next time the dressing needed changing.

"If you're a good girl today and let the doctor take your bandage off, I'll give you an ice cream cone," the nurse said.

"No!" Sylvia said, so the nurse sat at the end of the bed and ate the cone herself. Jim's daughter didn't have her gauze wrap changed that day.

Sylvia acknowledged she was not a model patient.

"I was the terror of the ward. I went from kid to kid, passing out things. We were monsters."

She still has memories of nurses using a toothbrush to get the BBs out of her skin — without local anesthetic. That procedure "hurt like heck," and she still has two or three BBs in her arm seven decades later.

Sylvia has forgiven her brother for pulling the trigger but not for something else he did after the hospital released her. When Air Force friends of her father passed through Camp Drake en route to deployments elsewhere, they often stopped at the Muri house for dinner. Aware of Sylvia's ordeal, someone brought her a treat that was novel then, colored marshmallows. Her parents, however, said she had to wait until the next day to try the sugary novelty.

When she got up in the morning, she saw an empty bag.

"Jim (her brother) found them and ate every one of them."

Her father turned the revolvers over to the military police, because "he didn't want them in the house anymore," Sylvia said.

Jim had the revolvers the previous October and used them to complete his convincing costume for his first Halloween in Japan. Six-foot-four with dark hair, he dressed up as the Lone Ranger, a pair of six-shooters holstered on his hip.

Long healed from the accidental gunshot wound, Sylvia has kept lifetime memories of her family's stay in Japan.

"It was a very colorful time in our lives. The more extraordinary it is, the easier you remember things," Jim and Alice Muri's

209

daughter, now 74, said in March 2019.

Chapter 18 - A Time of Transition

The Muris returned to the United States in the spring of 1950 and began a transitory time. Jim got about a month's leave and then the Air Force told him to report to Maxwell Air Force Base in Montgomery, Ala., for special training that lasted a few months. Next, he and his family headed to Washington state for MAT (Military Advisory Team) duty at McChord Air Force Base, south of Tacoma. His responsibilities involved coordinating the shipment of supplies to U.S. troops fighting in the Korean War.

After the McChord assignment ended, Jim and Alice returned to Florida, this time with their two children, and lived at 345 Plymouth Road in in Palm Springs. Jim served as director of material for Palm Beach International Airport, and while in that role, in early February 1952, the Air Force promoted him from major to lieutenant colonel, according to the *Palm Beach* (FL) *Post* (February 9, 1952).

When Jim's two-year stint in Palm Springs ended, the Muris yanked up their belongings again for a move west to Kelly Air Force Base in San Antonio. The Muris lived in "the Cabbage Patch," as they called it, a housing area next to the runways.

"Take good care of the kids. I'll be gone again for a while," Jim said at the end of one day as he strode into the Muris' home at Kelly, took off his Air Force coat, and hung it up, before turning to face his wife's inquiring look.

"How long will you be gone?" Alice asked. "What will you be doing?"

Questions tumbled out as Alice, who had been a military spouse for a decade, again faced the prospect of having a husband ordered to complete unknown tasks in unknown places by an organization with as much — or more — claim on him as his wife.

"I'm not sure. The brass aren't saying much. They want me to do some scouting for overseas bases."

World War II had ended seven years earlier, and international tensions were rising again. In August 1949, the Soviet Union had conducted its first successful test of an atomic weapon at a site in one of the USSR's Asian republics. Fears of another war grew in 1950; on June 25, North Korea, allied with its fellow Communist neighbor, China, invaded South Korea following border clashes. That started a war, which President Truman called a "police action," involving 21 United Nations members. The U.S. provided about 90 percent of the military personnel in the conflict. An armistice signed on July 27, 1953, ended fighting but not the dispute, which continues to this day.

Jim had seen Air Force planes and crews, headed for Korea, come through McChord and sensed the thinking in Washington.

"They think we've got to be ready in case the Commies attack. One Pearl Harbor is enough," said the pilot who had firsthand experience with the Japanese attack and its aftermath.

Jim was gone for a brief period; family members say it probably was at least two weeks, perhaps a month.

James Muri, 9 at the time, said in a 2019 Facebook message he heard stories of his father traveling on Air Force business to various parts of Africa. The itinerary may have also included the Caribbean and parts of Southeast Asia.

"He mentioned Trinidad and the orangutans stealing golf balls off the fairways," James wrote.

Orangutans are native only to Sumatra and Borneo, so Jim may have incorrectly identified primates found in Trinidad, James said.

"A Montana farm kid could easily make that sort of mistake. [However], if during his trip he visited Sumatra and/or Borneo, maybe not."

Jim's daughter, Sylvia, said she remembered hearing a story about her father visiting Portugal where he, as a chain smoker, couldn't use a cigarette lighter; the country banned the devices because match-making was a key part of the Portuguese economy.

"Funny what we remember," she mused almost 70 years later.

Also, she shared an unverified story of her father's co-pilot carrying a monkey inside his Air Force flight jacket back to the U.S.

"We're going overseas again," Jim told Alice in the spring of 1954 after the Air Force notified him he was to be transferred to NATO headquarters in Brussels. He joined the Military Assistance Advisory Group (MAAG) as a military attaché. Attaches represented all branches of the military in the group's work.

The stay in Belgium presented Jim with the next challenges of his life, professionally and personally.

On the professional front, he reported to a colonel he didn't respect. The man was a reserve officer, and Jim, an active-duty officer, resented the other man's command role, Sylvia said, adding there were other superiors who rubbed Jim the wrong way, too.

Unrelated to the command structure, as far as she knows, Jim's blood pressure soared while he was in Europe.

Fortunately, he got medical care, because the blood pressure situation was spotted during a routine physical exam or because Alice noticed the symptoms and they so alarmed her she called a doctor, or both. The Air Force sent Jim to the famed U.S. military hospital in Wiesbaden, Germany, Sylvia said in 2019.

Before his hospitalization, she said, "it got so bad he was taking glycerin tablets when he got home at nighttime. He would sit down in his easy chair after getting home from work — he was working six days a week, (with) only Sundays off."

Within a half hour of getting home and relaxing, "his face would turn red, and his eyeballs would turn red. That's how bad his blood pressure was," Sylvia said, recalling memories from when she was in elementary school.

"It wasn't happy duty for him because you were there for diplomatic reasons, and some of the people you were having to be diplomatic with weren't necessarily your favorite people."

The culture of the time played into Jim's ailment. He shouldn't have been drinking because of his elevated blood pressure, but he was. Alcohol consumption in party settings had been part of his military upbringing almost since when he enlisted, and the environment at NATO headquarters encouraged that lifestyle.

Both Jim and Alice, however, decided at some point that the cocktail scene was no longer for them because it centered on protocol.

"My mom hated that crap, and Dad got to the point where he did, too, because it was go over and pay the proper attention to the person who was higher in rank than you," Sylvia said.

Jim left the power games at NATO functions behind for a while at Wiesbaden, where excellent doctors cared for him. Still, his appearance shocked the first physician who walked into Jim's room and examined him.

"He said, 'Oh, my God, you scared me with those eyes,'" Sylvia said, explaining how the doctor reacted to his first sight of Jim's "light spooky eyes," accented by his ruddy complexion.

Jim survived mostly on yogurt while he was in the hospital. He underwent a series of tests and probably exercised during a stay of between two and four weeks.

When he was discharged and came home, he was chewing gun, which Sylvia had never seen him do before. He was following his doctor's orders.

" 'Chew gum and cuss out your wife once in a while. Don't eat too much salt and you'll be fine,' " the doctor said, according to Jim's daughter.

Jim put that episode behind him and was free of high blood pressure for several decades until his advanced years after he and Alice returned to Montana.

During his three-year deployment with NATO in Belgium, Jim missed one of the watershed moments in many people's lives during their late 30s: attending a 20-year reunion of one's high school graduating class, in his case, Custer County High School's Class of 1936.

A classmate, Dorothy Gibbs Muzio, tracked Jim down and wrote to him in 1956; his reply, found decades later, does not specifically mention a reunion, but Muzio may have sent an invitation.

Jim wrote back with an update on his life. He said he had been married 15 years, and he and his wife had a son and a daughter.

"During the past twenty years, I have spent my time traveling around the world with the Air Force. During all my travels, I don't believe I have run into any (members) of our graduating class."

Jim said he hoped to retire soon and take up "a lifetime of

hunting and fishing" — with no travel.

Back from Belgium in 1957, the Muris stopped in Carterville to visit Jim's parents on their way to another destination. It was late spring in Eastern Montana, and one of James' uncles decided it was time to introduce a greenhorn to a ranch ritual.

"It's time to go branding the new calves," the uncle said. The extended family mounted horses and headed toward what the Muris called "the boondocks," the badlands and breaks north of cultivated farmland along the Yellowstone River.

"And the branding started," James recalled in a conversation 60 years later.

"I was 13, and I knew what branding was. But what I didn't know was it also included dehorning, cutting [castration] and all that. And it all took about 30 seconds per steer; it was fast."

James and Sylvia's uncles thought it hilarious that their city cousins were getting their first look at what their rural kin grew up with. They persuaded James to get on a steer, which promptly threw him off, much to the delight of onlookers.

James learned about something else that day by watching the steer testicles being cut and thrown into a pot of boiling water. The adult Muri men, however, did something odd. They kept the tip of the steer sacs and put them in their pockets.

"After all the damage was done, and the steers were turned loose, we headed back to the ranch.

"When we got back, one of my uncles was pulling out all the little ends of the bags. I said, 'Why do you keep those?'"

The uncle replied, "So we know how many steers we have."

That answer didn't satisfy James.

"I said, well, you collected all the testicles. Why don't you just

216

count those and divide by two? And he said, it's easier, you don't have to do no arithmetic.

"I'm sure he was kidding me, but it made a helluva good story. He said it with a straight face."

Did James ever try a Western delicacy in some circles: Rocky Mountain oysters, prepared by boiling steer testicles, then coating them in floor and deep-fat-frying them?

"Absolutely not!" James said.

A Dallas base became Jim's final Air Force assignment. He and Alice moved a family that now included children approaching adolescence, to Texas, and Jim reported to the Dallas Naval Air Station, a facility known today as the Grand Prairie Armed Forces Complex.

The Dallas NAS began in 1929 as Hensley Field, a training field for reserve pilots of the Army Air Corps. It passed from Air Force command to the Navy in 1949, but the Air Force continued to use the field to train reserve pilots.

In late 1958, just before his retirement, Jim became involved in one of Dallas' iconic events: the annual Cotton Bowl festivities on New Year's Day. He helped coordinate an appearance by the Air Force Drum and Bugle Corps in the Cotton Bowl parade.

That year's Cotton Bowl football game featured a matchup between the Texas Christian University Horned Frogs, from neighboring Fort Worth, and the Air Force Falcons, representing the country's newest military academy, which was established in 1954 and graduated its first class in 1959. The January 1, 1959, bowl game ended in a scoreless tie, the first deadlock in 11 years, and it was the first Cotton Bowl broadcast on CBS, which televised thirty-eight of the next forty-one games.

A thank-you note from parade committee chairman Joe Skinner followed the bugle corps' appearance. In a note mailed to Muri, then director of material for the 2596 Air Force Base Squadron, Skinner said that without Muri's help, "We would have been out in left field without a glove with the sun in our eyes."

It was time for Jim to hang up his Uxbridge Blue Air Force uniform. Retirement orders sent from Air Force headquarters in Washington said Lieutenant Colonel Muri was relieved from assignment at the Dallas Naval Air Station on October 1, 1959. He could proceed to his "home of selection," in Air Force parlance, to complete his final paperwork. After 23 years in uniform, a tenure broken only when he worked for a farm-equipment manufacturer in South Dakota, Jim was a civilian again.

It's not known where Jim finalized his exit from the Air Force; he may have returned to March Field for that formality. He and Alice also had family matters to consider. Their son James, a typical "military brat" who attended 14 schools through high school, was nearing the end of the 12th grade. He graduated in a class of 66 students from the second high school he attended, Henley High in Klamath Falls, Oregon, in 1961.

Jim got a shock in 1963 when he heard about the sudden death of his best friend from the 22nd Bomb Group, Jo Jo Dewan, who was in his mid-40s when he succumbed to a heart attack. Sylvia, who graduated from high school in Riverside that year, said in 2019 that the news of Dewan's passing had "a huge impact" on her father because it stirred "his inner ghosts."

Jim and Alice knew what it felt like to be empty-nesters as they watched first James, then Sylvia finish high school, enter college, begin careers, marry and start families and go on to lives of their own. About then, Jim's flight at Midway attracted attention from authors writing books dealing about the Pacific phase of World War II or specifically about the battle.

The first to shine a spotlight on Jim's flight in Susie-Q was Martin Caidin, whose 1966 book, "The Ragged, Rugged Warriors," includes a chapter titled "The Other Midway." After a paragraph that places the reader at Midway, at dawn on June 4, 1942, Caidin continues:

"The light glistened on four short-wing killers, beneath which hung the ominous shapes of long torpedoes. The bombers were four Marauders of the 22nd and 38th Bomb Groups, assigned to Navy control on Midway to be used against the most powerful naval armada ever assembled. The Marauders were the only bombers in the AAF to mount the sleek torpedoes and this was to be the morning of their baptism."

In the spring of 1966, renowned author Walter Lord visited Jim and Alice while they lived at 4166 Saint Paul Place in Riverside. Lord was researching the Battle of Midway, collecting accounts from American and Japanese veterans and official reports of both militaries, for what became his 1976 classic, "Incredible Victory — The Battle of Midway."

When Lord returned to New York, he or an assistant typed a thank-you note to the Muris. Lord mentioned having a "fine lunch" with Jim and Alice, which gave him a "wonderful oasis" during a long day that didn't ended until got back to Los Angeles at 1 a.m.

Lord's letter also discussed three Japanese veterans he interviewed for the book, each of whom had a possible personal connection to Jim.

There was Admiral Ryunosuka Kusaka, Admiral Nagumo's Chief of Staff, who was on the Akagi, "and you gave him quite a scare with that B-26 attack. He specifically asked me for the name of the pilot who almost crashed the Akagi's bridge, and I think it would be most appropriate if you wrote and told him about Herbie Mayes," the pilot whose doomed, out-of-control B-26 angled across the carrier deck and crashed into the Pacific.

Lord also mentioned Juzo Mori, who was a torpedo plane pilot in the battle and thus had something in common with Muri. Mori, who operated a bar in Tokyo when Lord found him, was "most delightful."

Lord said he conversed with Raita Ogawa, who was part of the combat air patrol over the Japanese carriers. Ogawa "probably spent some of his time shooting at you," so he and Muri also had an apparent bond, Lord said.

Lord shared addresses for the three Japanese men and said Jim might enjoy corresponding with them. There is no evidence he did.

Chapter 19 - Back Home

Jim and Alice wanted a simpler life away from the hubbub of Air Force bases, many close to big cities. The opportunity came in 1970. They stayed briefly in Laurel, Montana, where Andy, Jim's brother and fellow World War II military pilot, lived and sold real estate, Sylvia recalled in 2019. Jim and Alice used a Laurel motel as their base as they scouted property in the region to buy with Andy's help. They found what they were looking for in late summer that year, a five-acre ranch on Bridger Creek between Reedpoint and Big Timber in the south-central part of the state; this became their home for the next 30 years.

Jim and Alice's ranch lay just inside the eastern boundary of Sweetgrass County, and an off-ramp from Interstate 90 provided convenient access to Big Timber and Reedpoint, in Stillwater County. Farther east along I-90, Montana's largest city, Billings, offered all the retail and medical care options the couple would need if they couldn't be gotten in Reedpoint and Big Timber.

Leading a less-hectic life was an idea — a goal — that incubated for years in the Muris' minds. As early as 1946, right after World War II ended and when Jim was working for International Harvester while waiting for his peacetime commission in the Army Air Force, he and Alice thought about alternatives to the military, according to their daughter.

Jim might have surprised Alice, though, with his desire to return to the military "because they had talked about getting a small acreage and having a farming life … not necessarily (in) Montana," Sylvia said, recalling her parents' retirement.

"That was kind of in the back of their head as a retreat. I don't think they expected to spend all their young years" as a couple focused on advancing Jim's career in the military.

Her parents, in their late 20s when the war ended, had come through that turbulence and then had no clear plan for life other than surviving the chaos they and millions of other Americans had witnessed. Twenty-five years later, the Muris had time to relax, surrounded by the beauty of Montana's Crazy Mountains to the north and the lofty Beartooth Range to the south. The majestic Yellowstone River flowed within walking distance of their place.

"If this isn't paradise, I don't know what is," Alice said to Jim as she planted flowers outside their log house on Bridger Creek and made it their home.

It didn't take long for Jim and Alice's ranch, in the heart of the Treasure State, to become a mecca for family members — brothers and sisters from Miles City, nieces and nephews starting careers in various Montana towns and cities or attending college in Bozeman and Missoula, and out-of-state relatives and friends who wanted to see the state.

For example, Alice's mother, Anne Moyer, traveled from Riverside to visit in September 1971. It was her first trip to Montana, and she was enjoying the state, according to a brief item in the *Big Timber Pioneer* (September 16, 1971), which typifies how grass-roots news appeals to readers of small-town newspapers in Montana and other states.

The Muris were becoming part of their new community by late summer 1970, according to the *Pioneer* (Sept. 17, 1970), which reported Alice's attendance as a guest at the first Kent Kommunity Klub meeting of the year.

Jim got unwelcome publicity in 1972. He was convicted in Big Timber police court of driving while intoxicated and fined $210, according to the *Pioneer* (March 30, 1972). This conviction apparently resulted from a March 25, 1972, accident in which he drove a pickup off Montana Highway 13 east of Big Timber into a barrow pit, where the vehicle turned over on its top. The *Pioneer* reported that a passerby helped Muri right the pickup; there was little damage, and he was not injured.

"Did you see? James got in the paper," Alice said to her husband one day in November 1973, referring to their son, who had achieved the rank of second lieutenant in the Army after serving as a medic in the Vietnam War. The item in the *Pioneer* (Nov. 8, 1973) said he and other American and Allied troops took part in Exercise Reforger V in Germany. Like his father, James was involved in military logistics — the exercise involved an airlift of about 11,000 U.S.-based soldiers and more than 1,000 tons of equipment to three airfields to prepare for the event. His regular duty was as a fire detection officer for the 3rd Infantry Division's 41st Artillery at Bad Kissingen, Germany. By the mid-1970s, the Army stationed him at Fort Bragg.

Jim and Alice settled into a life highlighted by having family members and friends stop for visits at holidays or if they needed to take a break on long drives across Montana. Jim's advice to those who knew him was, "I'm done traveling. If you want to see me, you have to come here," Sylvia recalled in a 2019 email.

She heeded those orders, driving each summer to Montana from Chico, California, each summer with her three daughters, while her husband, Ron, stayed home to run the country western bar they owned. The Saadati daughters and their mother stayed at Alice and Jim's place in Reedpoint, explored the surroundings and took part in Fourth of July picnics where they got to know their large Treasure State family.

A highlight of the Muris' retired life came forty-four years after the Battle of Midway on the day in the summer of 1976 when Jim figuratively redid his mission in a Billings movie theater. Hollywood brought the June 1942 event to the silver screen with a movie still praised today for its realism and general factual accuracy — except for the love story within the larger narrative. "Midway" featured an all-star cast: Charlton Heston, Henry Fonda, James Coburn, Glenn Ford, Hal Holbrook, Robert Mitchum, Cliff Robertson and Robert Wagner.

Heston portrayed a fictional Capt. Matt Garth. Actors who portrayed real individuals on the American side were Fonda (Admiral Chester Nimitz), Coburn (Capt. Vinton Maddox), Ford (Rear Admiral Raymond Spruance), Holbrook (Commander Joseph Rochefort), Mitchum (Admiral William Halsey), Robertson (Commander Carl Jessop) and Wagner (Lt. Commander Ernest L. Blake). Robert Webber had a smaller role as Rear Admiral Frank "Jack" Fletcher. Japanese actors who depicted key battle figures for their nation included Toshiro Mifune (Admiral Isoroku Yamamoto), James Shigota (Vice Admiral Chuichi Nagumo) and Robert Ito (Commander Minoru Genda).

The 1976 move (still available on DVD) alludes to the four-plane, B-26 attack on the Japanese fleet and the decision-making conundrum it helped caused among top Japanese commanders without mentioning or showing *Susie-Q* and the other Martin Marauders in Jim Collins' formation.

The movie came to Billings in June 1976 and showed at the downtown World Theater, which no longer exists. An advertisement for "Midway" in the *Billings Gazette* promised viewers a "Sensurround" experience: "The sights, sounds and actual sensations of combat. So real you can feel it."

Jim jumped at the prospect of reliving the battle; he and Alice drove seventy miles to Billings and saw the movie on June 19, 1976.

"I told my wife ... goddam, I gotta see that picture," Jim told *Gazette* columnist Addison Bragg, who interviewed him after he watched the movie.

He said Hollywood's version of the epic battle that became his life-shaping experience was "beautiful," and added:

"They stuck to the facts. The sound made you feel like you were right back there again. It was exciting — and even more so because I knew I could get up and walk out of there when it was all over."

Bragg's article described Jim as enjoying life as he neared his 60th birthday. "I've got five acres, a log home, three steers, three pigs and a big garden. We looked all over for a place to retire — and this is what we wanted."

Jim said he kept in touch with Susie-Q's co-pilot, Pren Moore, then living in El Centro, California, but he had lost track of the rest of No. 1391's crew.

Muri said the way his life had turned out satisfied him. "If I had it to do all over again, I wouldn't change a thing," he said, including the B-26 flight from Midway, skimming the deck of the Akagi and the harrowing return to Midway inside a bullet-riddled bomber that was carrying injured crew members to safety.

Three of Jim's brothers set up real estate offices in Montana in the post-war years, Buck in Miles City, Bill in Forsyth and Andy in Laurel. Jim followed their lead when he returned to the Treasure State. He got his real-estate license and became a broker in the

225

Reedpoint and Big Timber areas. He specialized in buying and selling ranch properties in south central Montana.

After he retired, Jim found time to travel more often to where he grew up. First, he and Alice drove from southern California; later, the trip was much shorter, from their home on Montana's Bridger Creek. The destination was the same in both instances: the home place, R.P. and Nellie Muri's ranch in the Eastern Montana community of Carterville.

There, with the undammed Yellowstone River flowing to the south and the rugged breaks and badlands of the Big Open country to the north, a master storyteller was in his element.

On a warm day, children from his large, extended family would gather around Jim. The younger ones were grandchildren, and Jim and Alice's older nieces and nephews sometimes joined the crowd. When the youngsters took a break from play, they gravitated toward someone who they had become used to delivering entertainment almost as good as TV or the movies.

"Grandpa ... Uncle Jim." The voices rang out. "Tell us a story. Mom and Dad said you flew airplanes in the war."

"Yes, I did. What should I tell you about today?" Jim said, scrunching his bushy eyebrows in simulated deep thought.

"Did you bring your airplane with you this time?" one awed listener asked.

"Sure!"

"Where is it?"

"I parked it on the other side of that hill," he said with a wink he hoped the children didn't notice as he pointed to the north. As he motioned, Jim felt a twinge of sadness about having his time as a pilot end two decades earlier.

"Let's go see it," shouted one kid, running toward the bluff. The others followed.

Momentary peace descended on the yard, broken only by the sound of a meadowlark singing on a post and the buzz of mosquitoes.

Soon, though, the troop of plane hunters returned to where Jim was chatting with his brothers, sisters and the teens and young adults.

"Grandpa," exclaimed one of the expedition members, "there's no plane there. You pulled our leg again."

Jim smiled.

"Guess I did, but all of you needed to burn off some energy. Like I did when I was your age, trying to catch wild horses in the badlands. Did I ever tell you about … ?"

Chapter 20 – *Susie-Q* Returns to the Air(waves)

Over three decades after Jim Muri buzzed the deck of Akagi with his B-26, his bomber took to the air again.

Except this time Muri wasn't at the controls of *Susie-Q*. And he wasn't making a dash for his life and his crew's lives, trying to find the airstrip at Midway amid the expanse of the Pacific Ocean. And, when this imaginary trip occurred, Muri wasn't aware of it, even though it happened about 60 miles from the ranchette where he and Alice retired at the flank of the Montana's lofty Beartooth Range.

What happened in the 1970s was a flight of fancy, a song crafted by a fellow World War II veteran, a Navy flight crewman from West Virginia who gained national fame as a country music broadcaster for several radio stations in Billings, Montana.

"Midway" was the name of the song. Its composer, who recorded the ballad and has sung it during his country music radio show and on other occasions, was Lonnie Bell.

"I think I wrote the song about 1976. I wrote it before the movie (Midway, released in the summer of 1976) came out," Bell said in a 2017 interview, before his 93rd birthday.

Bell came to Billings in 1964 and was a fixture for decades in Montana's largest city and throughout its vast trade region. He worked for several radio stations and hosted a show every Sunday morning on KGHL for 33 years before he retired in April 2018.

Bell became a legend in country music circles, where he crossed paths with dozens of headliners. He may be best known for giving Kentuckian Loretta Lynn, of "Coal Miner's Daughter" movie

229

fame, her break into music recording when he ran dances in a rented hall in Anacortes, Washington. Bell first heard Lynn sing in the basement of the American Legion club in Bellingham, Washington, 60 miles away. Bell was an announcer for KGAT in Anacortes and while there, "I was the first guy to ever play a Loretta Lynn record on the radio." The country music legend's lasting appreciation for Bell caused her to always refer to him as "the man who discovered me," according to Bell's autobiography.

Bell's accomplishments earned him a spot in the Country Music Disc Jockey Hall of Fame, and in 2002 he won the national Golden Voice Award for "radio personality of the year." Despite the accolades, listener involvement remained a priority for Bell; people were encouraged to call in requests to play songs on his radio show.

Bell spent 20 years in the Navy and got his start in radio in 1953 while still in the military. He was stationed in Hawaii after the war, and a DJ in Oahu invited him to help spin records at the station.

After he became a Billings radio personality, Bell said he heard from "a couple guys that called whose dads were killed" at Midway. What inspired him to pen his Midway song, though, was the country's wrenching experience in the Vietnam War, which ended with a truce only about three years before.

"The reason I wrote this song (is that) I was watching TV, and this one veteran was (testifying before) Congress. He was a sergeant. He slammed his fist against the table and told the congressmen, damn it, we all want to put ourselves besides the World War II veterans.

"I wrote the song for him" and in memory of someone else. "My son-in-law was killed in Vietnam. He was an Army cook."

Bell, despite his Navy service, knew his song couldn't concentrate on the glories of that branch's record at Midway in 1942 and exclude other servicemen who played vital roles in the battle.

"I said if I write a song about Midway, I'll have to include those Air Force fellas. I don't want to say it was all Navy," he said, adding his opinion that Nimitz and Admiral Bill "Bull" Halsey, "all of them didn't accept (the) Air Force" contribution to victory.

"So, I wrote (about) this plane called 1391, that was the number. Jim Muri was 23 at the time. He was the commander of that flight. However, I didn't know him.

"So, I write this song. And the line goes, 'From the *Hornet* came Torpedo 8 and 1391 came from the island of Midway to meet the Rising Sun. ' " (Torpedo 8 was the Navy squadron decimated by the Japanese.)

A quarter-century passed. Then, in the early 2000s, chance circumstances brought Bell and the man his song referred to without naming him — Jim Muri — together in Billings. That happened after Jim and Alice moved there because hospitals there could better meet her health needs. Alice died just before her 80th birthday in 2001, and Jim continued to live in their house on Avenue F on the city's West End.

Bell described what happened next, a sequence of events involving his friend Don Cooper, whose daughter, Kristie, is married to Yellowstone County commissioner John Ostlund. Don and Kristie are accomplished musicians with records to their credit, which Bell played on his show.

"One day, (Kristie) was cleaning houses on Avenue F. I don't think you can get any sharper than she is. She's running the vacuum cleaner in this old gentlemen's house. She knows my song because we're close friends.

"She looks and sees this picture (Roy Grinnell's "A Shot Across the Bow," a painting of *Susie-Q* buzzing the deck of Akagi, signed by Muri and a copy of which the artist had given to him). She says that's 1391 — that's the plane Lonnie sings about. She looks at this old man sitting in his chair and says, 'Whose plane is that?'"

Bell, imitating the gruffness of Jim's speech in his advanced age, gave the Marauder Man's response: "That's my plane."

Kristie Ostlund's response was dramatic.

"She jumps straight in the air. She says, do you know Lonnie Bell? He says, 'Oh, yeah, I've heard of him. My little wife used to listen to him.' He always referred to his wife as 'my little wife.' "

Ostlund got the ball rolling. She told her father what had happened when she cleaned Jim's house. And Cooper's reaction didn't mince words, according to Bell.

"Don said, 'You gotta be puttin' me on.' Don says, 'Take me over there.' Don's the friendliest guy in the world, but he just goes charging over there, and he introduces himself to Jim.

"He says, 'Do you know Lonnie Bell?' And Jim says, 'Yeah, I've heard of him but I don't know him. Them cowboys don't know anything about the war, so I didn't bother to get hold of him.' So, Cooper jumps straight in the air. I was his hero; I've known him since he was 18."

Cooper told Jim a little about Bell's wartime record, embellishing the account by describing him as having been "in charge of naval operations" and having taken part in the Battle of Midway.

(Bell, who enlisted in the Navy in 1940 at age 16, was a crewman on a Navy PBY Catalina scout plane. As a second mechanic, he started the plane's engine from inside, a procedure that required him to climb into the tower where the starter was located. His unit flew patrols from New Caledonia in the Southwest Pacific in early 1942 and while there, they heard about Jimmy Doolittle's April 1942 raid on Tokyo. Bell's PBY later saw the U.S. aircraft carrier *Lexington* from the air just before the Battle of the Coral Sea in early May 1942. When the Battle of Midway occurred from June 4-6, 1942, Bell and his fellow PBY airmen were flying patrol duty from Hawaii. There they heard about the battle from Navy and Army fliers in conversations that included the story of the B-26 pilots and crews that attacked the Japanese fleet.)

Cooper asked the man he had just met, "Can I bring him (Bell) over? So old man Muri says, 'All right. Bring him over.'"

Cooper may have been convinced he had found the Army pilot in the "Midway" lyrics, but Bell needed convincing.

"So, Cooper comes running up to the radio station and he says, 'I found the guy that was flying 1391.' I said, what bar did you find him in? Cooper says, 'No, he's for real.' He takes me over there," Lonnie said.

That prompted a lively exchange between the two World War II veterans.

"He starts asking questions. The next thing you know, me and him was locking horns. Two of the greatest friends in the world."

To compound the irony, Jim and Lonnie could have met in the 1970s and 1980s when they frequented the same Treasure State surroundings. In 1971, Jim and Alice had settled on their five-acre place on Bridger Creek, near the Stillwater-Sweet Grass county line in south-central Montana. A few years earlier, Lonnie began "cowboying" during a cattle drive on Bridger Creek and became a regular presence as a horseback rider there and in the nearby towns of Reedpoint and Big Timber.

In his autobiography, the affable broadcaster told how he adopted the Montana ethos not long after he came to the state. In the spring of 1964, he met a waitress, Peggy Todd, who worked at Billings' landmark Seventeen Club. She was the daughter of a rancher who lived in Reedpoint, the community Jim and Alice Muri would join a few years later.

Bell helped Todd move items from her aunt's house in Reedpoint to Billings and thus got to know her family. Peggy Todd's brother, Don, gave Bell a refresher course in horseback riding, which led the Todds to invite him to join them on their annual cattle drive. This involved moving the family herd from winter pastures in the Yellowstone River Valley to summer range in the foothills of the Beartooth Mountains. The event started every year on July 16, two days after cowboys and cowgirls, including Peggy Todd and her sister-in-law, Rosalie, gathered at the ranch.

Once underway, the drive went up Bridger Creek passing "several big beautiful ranches" and then followed a 40-mile trail along Lower Deer Creek, which Bell recalled having one ranch on it a half-century ago.

"The cattle moved at a swift pace until we reached a place called Tomato Can, where the cattle are left for the summer," he said.

Their friendship led Don Todd to give Bell a horse named Tom Thumb. In 1965, Lonnie and his horse began a tradition that made them legendary in the Reedpoint-Big Timber area. It was the annual March of Dimes fundraiser, done on horseback, which originated with Lonnie riding Tom Thumb in January 1965 from Reedpoint to Billings. His route took Bell along the partially completed I-90 and U.S. Highway 10 as he collected money for the charity during the 67-mile trip. It took 12 hours for Bell and his horse, both nearly frozen, to reach the Ox Bow Saloon in Billings on that cold Sunday. They got to the watering hole before 6 p.m., winning a bet on their arrival time with saloon owner Al Pearl, who paid off by buying drinks for the house.

The Todd family accompanied Lonnie on the second March of Dimes ride, which started a routine of annual January benefit rides on horseback from Reedpoint to Billings that ended in 1980. By then, Tom Thumb was 20 years old, traffic on I-90 was heavier, and it was dangerous to be riding a riding a horse on a freeway shoulder with cars and trucks whizzing by. Plus, "I was just too old to continue the long rides," said Lonnie, who turned 56 that summer.

March of Dimes organizers shortened the ride, which continued into the 1980s. For the 19th annual event in 1983, 24 riders collected $1,200 on a trip from a ranching community north of Big Timber into the Sweetgrass County seat. Lonnie, then a DJ for KOYN in Billings, rode with the group in the afternoon.

Thus, Bell became well known in the same Bridger Creek-Reedpoint community that the Muris called home for three decades. When they lived in their quiet rural retreat, Alice heard Bell on the radio and thought her husband should meet the radio personality.

Bell related in the 2017 interview what he heard later about Alice's urging Jim to meet Bell years before their paths crossed by chance after Alice's death.

Muri said his wife "told me one day you ought to go over and get acquainted with those boys," Bell and others who rode horses in the Bridger Creek area, according to Bell's recollection of what Kristie Ostlund told him about her first encounter with Jim Muri.

That prodding continued for about 20 years. Nothing happened. The Muris moved to Billings. Alice died just before her 80th birthday, and Jim became a widower for the final 12 years of his life. Thanks to the alertness of Kristie Ostlund, though, Muri met the songwriter who brought his flight to the airwaves, and they became friends for the final phase of Jim's life.

The circle of friends soon expanded when Lonnie introduced another of his friends, Roger Nelson, to Jim. Nelson, a former crop duster, had logged 24,000 hours as a pilot. He and Bell took Muri to lunch in Billings.

"Muri says, 'I lived on Bridger Creek for 30 years,'" Bell said.

Bell repeated that statement, then delved deeper into the ties he had, unknown until then, with Muri.

"I said I used to cowboy up there when I first came to Montana. I used to go up there with Don Todd, and we'd go up Fort Creek and take 250 head of cattle down into the head of Bridger Creek. And he said, 'Yeah, you went right by my house.' And I said, 'Are you the military guy that lived there?' He said, 'Yeah.'"

One day, as Todd and Bell rode side by side in the Beartooth foothills, they passed the Muri place. "I asked him who lived there, and he said, 'Some old sour head who retired from the military.' He laughed," Lonnie said.

Bell said that when he wrote Midway, the B-26 pilot it acclaimed could have been living anywhere in the world.

"Can you imagine? I got that number (1391, Susie-Q's identifier) out of a book. Can you imagine the guy being from Billings (late in his life) and me writing that song? There were 16 million people in World War II. What was the odds of that happening?"

Nelson's role in the friendship between Muri and Bell began in the early 2000s, when Kristie Ostlund was cleaning Muri's house. One day, her son accompanied his mother to the house. That was the day when Ostlund saw the Grinnell painting and asked Muri about it.

Before the Ostlunds left that day, Jim gave Kristie's son something to remember him by, a set of his Air Force wings, which Jim asked the youth to give to his grandfather, Don Cooper. Cooper asked the youngster where he got the wings.

"Oh, I got 'em when mom was cleaning Jim Muri's house," his grandson replied.

That prompted Cooper to call Bell, who called Nelson, one of Bell's longtime friends, and drew him into the circle. Nelson stopped at Jim's house, met him and took him to lunch with Bell and Cooper at Gussick's, a popular Billings steakhouse. Nelson and Muri swapped flying stories.

"He started telling about the bullet holes (in Susie-Q) and all this stuff. So, I tell him, I've got thousands of hours in the air. I've had electrical storms, hailstorms, engine fires, but I've never had anybody shoot at me," Nelson said.

"From that day, him and I clicked."

Midway, the tune that brought Lonnie and Jim together, lives on. Taylor Brown, president of Northern Broadcasting Co., KGHL's parent company, said the station still gets requests to play the song, especially on holidays special to military veterans and their families, such as Memorial Day and Veterans Day.

You can listen to Lonnie Bell's song on SoundCloud (free registration); use this link:

https://soundcloud.com/search?q=Midway%20Lonnie%20Bell

Chapter 21 - High Honors Late in Life

It became time for Jim to shut down his real-estate office and list his own place for sale. Alice's failing health prompted the couple's decision to move to Billings to get the medical care she needed. An advertisement in the *Big Timber Pioneer* (June 20, 1997) offered the Muri's five-acre place on Bridger Creek, consisting of a log home with a knotty pine and oak interior, a five-car garage and "much more." Jim and Alice found a buyer and moved to Billings.

On June 26, 2001, Jim lost his wife of almost 60 years. Alice died at Billings Deaconess Hospital from heart problems complicated by a broken hip, according to her obituary in the *Pioneer* (July 6, 2001).

The obituary mentioned Alice's skill in dealing with people.

"She was comfortable with four-star generals and ambassadors and was always ready with a smile or a joke," the article said, noting her service as a military wife who lived around the world and made it better.

Other memories collected for her print farewell included "her girlish giggle," her cooking ability and her love of reading and flower and vegetable gardening.

Still adjusting to life without his wife, Jim called Roger Nelson one day in 2003 and asked him to come over to Jim's house on the West End of Billings.

When Roger arrived, Jim showed him a letter he had received from Washington, D.C.

"Here, read this. They want me to come to Washington to pick up the Jimmy Doolittle Award, " Jim said.

But Roger was mistaken if he thought Jim would relish the chance to pick up an honor named for the man he had flown with one day during the war. As Roger recalled Jim's reaction to the letter:

"He said, 'I'm not going.' I said, what do you mean? He said, 'I can't go. Look at my knee. I can't get around. I've got a hernia.' "

Nelson pointed out that the airline would take good care of his veteran friend, then nearing his 85th birthday.

"You gotta go and pick up an award like this," Roger said.

Jim put up further resistance before saying he would think about the trip overnight.

"The next day he calls me and says, 'I will go to Washington on one condition. I'm going to make you my liaison officer. You handle the whole thing. Make the calls to Washington, set up the deal and talk to the president of the World War II committee and his assistant.' "

Thus delegated, Nelson took up his task. He worked with the committee to get plane tickets and room reservations and arranged other details. The two pilots were set for a trip to the capital.

Nelson brought along a recording of Lonnie Bell's "Midway," which played on the public address system at the Doolittle event in November 2003.

"We really had a history lesson with all those people telling stories," and someone piqued by Jim's story was a representative of *Ghost Wings* magazine. The publication published an article about Muri, after Jonathan Abbott, one of its writers, came to Billings and, assisted by Nelson, spent a few days interviewing Muri. The article, with Roy Grinnell's painting of Susie-Q's flight

("A Shot Across the Bow,") appeared in Issue 13 of the now-defunct magazine, published in the mid-2000s.

Jim barely had time to rest before he was invited back to the nation's capital. Jim and Roger attended the unveiling of the World War II Memorial on May 29, 2004.

Nelson said Navy veterans made up most of the audience at one function he and Muri attended. Nelson got Muri to "the front line with all the head boys that were in battle."

As he stood nearby, carrying Jim's copy of the Grinnell painting he had brought with him, Nelson drew someone's attention.

"He looks at this picture and says, 'What's this?' I say, it's the Battle of Midway, and this guy flew down the deck of the Akagi. He says, 'You gotta be kidding me.' I say, yeah, he's sitting right over there," Roger said, nodding in Muri's direction.

Nelson invited the man to meet Muri just as World War II Navy veteran and movie star Tony Curtis finished his speech. Curtis served on Navy submarines in the Pacific from September 1943 to December 1945.

"This guy's dad is standing next to Jim Muri. He (the son) says, 'Dad, look at this picture. This is the guy that flew down the deck.'"

"Where's Tony?" someone said and ran to get Curtis.

Reporters from three Washington television stations spotted Curtis talking to a veteran they knew nothing about. They converged on Curtis and Muri and interviewed the Hollywood personality and the Montana man for stories broadcast that night.

Jim received further acclaim in 2007 when he was inducted into the "Gathering of Eagles" at Maxwell Air Force base. He joined 15 others added to the "Eagles" list of distinguished military aviators during the 26th annual event in Montgomery, Alabama.

The observance began after Brig. Gen. Paul Tibbets, pilot of Enola Gay, the B-29 bomber that the dropped the world's first atomic bomb on Hiroshima, spoke at the Maxwell Air Command Staff College, according to the *Montgomery* (AL) *Advertiser* (June 7, 2007). Students and faculty created a program that would help future enrollees learn aviation history first-hand from flying greats.

Failing health forced Jim, then 89, to decline a trip to Alabama. Instead, a member of the 2007 class, Air Force Maj. Robert B. "Brian" Copes, traveled to Jim's home in Billings and interviewed him for his research report, "The Last Midway Marauder," which he submitted as part of requirements for his graduation.

"The opportunity to interact with a living aviation legend, Mr. James P. Muri, has been one of the high moments of my Air Force career and a part of my life that I will share with my children and their children," Copes wrote.

"Mr. Muri's life stories, along with his heroic act of courage on 4 June 1942 are incidents you read about in fiction novels or see in action scenes on the silver screen. However, in this case it is not fiction, but a true life account of the fortitude and guts it took for him to fly down the deck of the Japanese carrier *Akagi* ..."

Copes said Muri's dramatic feat carries a deeper message applicable to modern military officers.

"His story is about leadership and how a man can be shaped by his surroundings to become a great leader of men. Although Muri was not an event-making figure, the way he dealt with challenges allowed him to showcase his leadership style."

Joining the "Eagles" put Muri in lofty company. The first gathering in 1982 included Tibbets, Doolittle, Curtis LeMay, Leigh Wade, and Neil Armstrong. Inducted as Eagles in later years were

George H.W. Bush, John Glenn, and Jeremiah Denton.

Chapter 22 - What the Battle Meant Then and Means Now

Anyone first hearing about Jim Muri's *Susie-Q* and the other three B-26s that attacked the Japanese fleet sailing toward Midway asks: If those Marauders did not hit a Japanese ship despite launching three torpedoes, how did Jim and his fellow Army fliers help win the battle?

Fair enough. People have been tackling that conundrum almost since the battle ended. At first the answer was easy. Torpedoes from the B-26s, skimming the ocean, and bombs from B-17 Flying Fortresses, soaring 20,000 feet above the Japanese ships, hit their targets in a combined punch that sunk at least one carrier. This mistaken thinking stemmed from initial confusion over what happened — what we now call the "fog of war." Also, likely to gain bragging rights in its inter-service rivalry with the Navy, the Army planted a stake in the ground at Hawaii. Our bombers, the high-flying B-17s and the water-hugging B-26s, scored hits against the Japanese with bombs and torpedoes, was the Army's thinking. These pilots and crews got back to Honolulu before the Navy fliers did, so the AAF got its story out first.

The Army-centric story was picked up by national radio —the Army Hour broadcast in June 1942 with a segment focused on the battle was a prime example — and by the *New York Times* and other leading national newspapers.

All that didn't sit well with members of the dive-bomber squadrons led by Wade McLuskey and Dick Best. When they and their carriers got back to Hawaii and heard the thunder of their smashing attack on the Japanese carriers stolen by the Army upstarts, it triggered heated arguments in Honolulu bars. Even some fisticuffs raged, according to accounts from the time.

Yet the Army-Navy squabbling, with Marine flyers and their sacrifice thrown in the mix for good measure, obscured one truth about the Battle of Midway. The B-26s, the Army's contribution to torpedo bombing on June 4, along with more than three dozen Navy torpedo planes, helped the U.S. triumph, but in a way more nuanced than a count of direct hits on enemy ships.

Early recognition of the torpedo bombers' role came from Harvard's Samuel Eliot Morison, a leading World War II historian who was a naval officer himself during the war years. Morison wrote that 41 torpedo planes took off from three U.S. carriers, and only six returned. None of them hit a ship. He didn't mention the B-26s, but their contribution to victory comes through in Morison's analysis.

"[I]t was the stark courage and relentless drive of those young pilots of the obsolete [Navy] torpedo planes that made possible the victory that followed.

"The radical maneuvering that they imposed on the Japanese carriers prevented them from launching more planes, and the TBDs by acting as magnets for the enemy's combat air patrol and pulling 'Zekes' down to near water level, enabled the dive-bombing squadrons that followed a few minutes later to attack virtually unopposed by fighter planes and to drop bombs on full deck loads in the process of being refueled."

More than 50 years after Morrison wrote those words, another expert not only reiterated the torpedo planes' key contribution to victory but also positioned the Midway battle outcome as crucial in a global context. This view came from James Schlesinger, former secretary of defense, former CIA director and former secretary of energy. His commentary appeared in the June 4, 2002, issue of the *Wall Street Journal*.

"Midway was one of the crucial battles, not only in World War II's and the nation's history but in world history," Schlesinger said.

Celebration of D-Day, when Allied troops hit the beaches of Normandy, is appropriate, he said, but by June 1944, Hitler was doomed. Two years earlier, Allied victory was far more uncertain before the U.S. prevailed after the June 4-6, 1942, clash in the Pacific.

"Indeed, it was Midway that in a sense made D-Day possible. Without Midway, the Allies could not have executed the overall strategy or victory in World War II."

Schlesinger wrote about the U.S.'s good fortune in having its carriers away from Pearl Harbor on December 7, 1941, and thus escaping being sunk or put out of action, the fate that befell eight U.S. battleships. Still, those U.S. carriers, when sent to Point Luck off Midway, launched slower and less maneuverable planes than the Japanese had, further handicapped by their ineffective torpedoes. Schlesinger included the B-26s in that statement regarding carrying the same semi-worthless torpedoes the Navy did, although the Marauders were high-performance bombers capable of speed equal to that of the Zeroes. Still, Muri, his crew and the other B-26 pilots and their crews sent to Midway received only a few hours of torpedo training and got no chance to launch a practice torpedo. They learned on the job on June 4th, so to speak, while dozens of Zeroes were attacking them and ship anti-aircraft fire filled the sky and shredded their aircraft.

"The battle was won through a combination of astonishing

courage, skill and good luck," combined with superior American intelligence exemplified by the code-breaking genius of Joseph Rochefort.

Listing the disadvantages the torpedo planes took into battle, Schlesinger said they had no fighter cover, were "painfully" slow and carried torpedoes that were inferior. Other than plane speed, the same drawbacks applied to Muri and the rest of the Marauder men at Midway. Plus, their B-26s, along with six Navy Avengers and inferior Marine planes, carried out the first direct attack against the Japanese fleet. Their mission, suicidal and sacrificial, put Admiral Nagumo in a decision-making quandary, a condition worsened by further torpedo plane attacks.

Japanese Zeroes shot down almost all the torpedo planes short of their targets, and none scored hits.

"But their self-sacrificing run created the basis for victory. They had brought the Japanese Combat Air Patrol down to sea level," Schlesinger said. That left Japanese Zeroes unable to defend when the Navy dive-bombers bolted in out of the blue."

To compound Japan's fatal problems, when the Enterprise's dive bombers arrived at mid-morning on June 4, Nagumo's men were preparing to launch more planes. Caught with their guard down, Navy dive bombers hit their mark and sank or damaged three carriers in a five minute attack. The one carrier in that trio still afloat, Soryu, retreated but sank that evening. More U.S. dive bombers hit the fourth Japanese carrier, Hiryu, on the afternoon of June 4, and she sank early the next day.

Even to this day, some purported experts on the Pacific Theater of World War II and the Battle of Midway either express ignorance of the B-26s' contribution to victory or deny it in favor of an all-

Navy version of the outcome.

There is, however, no denying this: Jim's Distinguished Service Cross and the DSCs earned by 27 other Marauder Men for their action on June 4, 1942, were deserved. Their bravery and heroism helped the U.S. win one of the greatest battles in world history.

Chapter 23 - Death Brings Further Accolades

Jim Muri's death on February 3, 2013, received widespread notice. Tom Howard, a *Billings Gazette* reporter who interviewed Jim several times in the final decade of his life, wrote about the man whose heroism remained newsworthy seventy years after it happened. That piece, along with an obituary placed by his family, appeared in newspapers across the U.S. and in several foreign newspapers and military publications and other news outlets geared towards veterans.

Muri's most prestigious obituary appeared in the *New York Times* on February 9, 2013. In an article headlined "James Muri, Bomber Pilot Honored for Valor in Battle of Midway, Is Dead at 94," *Times* reporter Paul Vittelo wrote that Muri "survived the first half of June 4, 1942, on the strength of his Army Air Forces pilot training." Vittelo explained to those unfamiliar with Muri's feat that it occurred during his first combat mission, on the first day of battle.

"He piloted an unwieldy B-26 twin-engine bomber through heavy anti-aircraft fire, maneuvered it close to a Japanese aircraft carrier, dropped a torpedo and pulled away into a sky filled with enemy shells just as his bomb detonated.

"He survived the second half of the day — getting back to base with three wounded crewmen on board — on the strength of a hunch," Vittelo wrote. He told readers about Muri's inspiration of swinging Susie-Q low over Akagi's deck to avoid her guns, which saved his life and that of his six crew members, .

The *Times* quoted Muri's son, James, on his father's legacy.

"I don't think he minded one bit not flying another mission," James said.

"It always surprised him a little that people even wanted to talk about it at all. I don't think he realized it was as big a deal as it was."

A story aired on National Public Radio (carried by Yellowstone Public Radio, based in Billings) featured an interview with Jim's daughter, Sylvia Saadati. This broadcast piqued the author's interest in Muri, a fellow Miles Citian.

Sylvia said her father's status as a hero of the battle surprised and embarrassed him.

"He simply wanted to be sent to Australia and be with his crew. But instead, he was held in the United States (after Midway) and written up and finally sent to Florida to help torpedo bombers," she told "Morning Edition" host Robert Siegel.

Sylvia added a personal note about the man she called dad for 68 years.

"He was the raconteur of the family. If you read one of his obituaries that my brother and my nephew and I sat around in a Billings bar and finalized, we put humor in there because we said maybe it wasn't always 100 percent true, but it certainly was fun to listen to.

"All of the different adventure stories of their (Jim and his siblings) growing up in Montana, etc.. So, I like to remember him with a group of kids sitting around him, telling stories," she said.

Today, Jim and Alice Muri lie in the Eastern Montana Veterans Cemetery. It sits on a gentle rise about a mile south of Miles City. The Yellowstone River meanders through the valley about 3-1/2 miles to the north. The fabled waterway remains the lifeblood for south-central and Eastern Montana, and because Jim gravitated to the Yellowstone throughout his life, it provides a fitting backdrop for his final resting place. Montana's second state cemetery for veterans encompasses 30 acres, with room for about 15,000 burials, according to the *Billings Gazette* (April 25, 2000).

Their repose puts the Muris puts them in the company of 250 veterans and their spouses, as of September 3, 2017, honored in a peaceful setting. The cemetery was dedicated on Memorial Day, May 28, 2001, in a ceremony that included a re-enactment of the flag-raising over Iwo Jima, site of another iconic World War II battle in the Pacific, as reported by the *Great Falls Tribune* (May 28, 2001).

Those honored range in age at the time of their death from 28-year-old Trevor Lee Quoroz, who served in the Navy in Iraq, to 102-year-old Clarence O. Worrall, an Army veteran of World War II. Jim Muri's longevity — he lived 94 years, 3 months, 15 days — puts him in the company of fellow Army vets Roy Volkman, who died 11 days before his 98th birthday, and Ervin Schmidt, 94 years, 7 months, 7 days old at his death.

Several members of Jim's large family still live in Miles City and can honor his memory. The cemetery draws a modest flow of visitors who pay respects to the men and women who took up arms or otherwise served their country.

Jim grew up on Eastern Montana's Great Plains and found his inspiration to fly in the wide open skies above the Yellowstone River. He got his wings, learned to fly the tricky B-26 bomber and became a hero of the Battle of Midway.

Surprised by fame, Jim avoided the spotlight and chose to live in rural Montana for most of the final four decades of his life. A century after his birth, a man from a humble background has been reclaimed by the Treasure State as one of its own, part of a legacy of service to country. And remembered as a story teller par excellence.

Appendix – Abbreviated Midway Chronology

Timeline courtesy of Marshall Magruder, who created it using Japanese and U.S. after-action reports. Wording inside curly brackets ({}) denotes Japanese reports; wording not enclosed in curly brackets is from U.S. reports. Information inside curly brackets that is italicized comes from Admiral Chuichi Nagumo's battle report.

BATTLE OF MIDWAY CHRONOLOGY FOR 4 JUNE 1942

0130-0230 Four PBY-5A night torpedo attack against {Transport Group, 1 hit}

0245   {Reveille on Japanese carriers, Reveille at 0300 on Midway}

0400   11 PBYs take off for search patrol, 16 B-17s for strike {on Transport Group}

0430   {VADM Nagumo commences launching 108 strike and reconnaissance planes}

0520   PBY reports an unidentified aircraft, {0530 sights an enemy aircraft carrier}

0545   PBY reports {"Many aircraft heading for Midway"}. Heard by Task Forces 16 & 17

0600   All Midway aircraft start launching, Avengers and B-26s are last launched.

0600   B-26 told to attack enemy ships, take off by 0615, {Midway attacked at 0630}

0700-0705   Hornet and Enterprise start launching (will attack from 1000 to 1025)

0705   Submarine Nautilus sees smoke on horizon {from AA, later strafed, depth bombed}

0705   {Lt Tomonaga radioed there is a need for second strike on Midway.}

0705   {Akagi sights 9} enemy planes {bearing 150 degrees, distance 25,000 meters, elevation 0.5 degrees. Assumed battle speed #5, heading into} the above mentioned planes.

0707   {Akagi commences firing with her starboard AA guns.}

0708   {About 10 friendly fighters head for the enemy.}

0710   {Three fighters take off from the Akagi. Enemy torpedo planes divide into two groups. [33 CAP (combat air patrol) are over the force]}

0711   {Akagi heads into the planes to starboard.}

0712   {Cruiser Tone sights a group of enemy planes heading for our carriers.} Three planes {heading for this ship [= Akagi] bearing 160 degrees to starboard, elevation 10 degrees.}

0712   {Akagi notes that enemy planes} loosed torpedoes. {Counters with AA machine gun fire.} Enemy machine gun strafing {seriously injures two men manning the #3 AA gun. Revolving mechanism of said gun damaged (repaired about half an hour later). Both transmitting antennas cut. Unable to use port ... (?).}

0712   {Akagi makes full turn to evade, successfully, the torpedo to starboard, and another full turn evades} another to port until 0716. Noted one torpedo to starboard, two to port (one exploded automatically) on parallel courses, and other crossed astern.

0712.5 {Hold main [8-inch and larger battleship and cruiser] battery gunfire. Commence AA gunfire.}

0713   {Air battle over the carriers.}

0715   Torpedo dropped ahead {of Akagi.}

0715   {Message from CinC First Air Fleet: "Planes in second attack wave stand by to carry out attack today. Re-equip yourselves with bombs."}

0716   {Cruiser Chikuma turns her main guns on} enemy planes {that were trying to escape friendly fighters.} Enemy planes {cut to three.}

0717   Three planes {brought down by AA fire.}

0726   {Akagi assumes battle speed #4. Ammunition box attached to her #2 machine gun damaged by machine gun fire. (Emergency repairs completed in about 10 minutes)}

0730-1000   B-17s, US Marine aircraft, two Torpedo squadrons {attack enemy carriers,} no hits.

~0745   {Vice-Admiral Naguno orders to unload torpedoes, upload anti-ship bombs.}

1025-1030   Navy Dive Bombers hit {three carriers.}

1200   Lt. Thornborough's B-26 launches torpedo at {Japanese carrier} off the Aleutian Islands, no hit.

Notes

INTRODUCTION

15   **Up to his full:** Telephone and personal interviews with Sylvia Saadati, at various times from 2013 through 2018.

15   **Screamed, whistled and scraped**: Albatross sounds at https://www.naturesoundmap.com/listing/laysan-albatross/

16   **to serve Army, Marine:** Robert J. Cressman et al., *A Glorious Page in Our History: The Battle of Midway 4-6 June 1942*, p. 15.

16   **to his wife, Alice:** James P. Muri, Letters from Jim Muri to Alice Muri (1941)

19   **As noted Midway author:** Walter Lord, *Incredible Victory: The Battle of Midway*, Chapter 1

CHAPTER 1

22   **Shallow-draft steamboats:** Steve McCarter, *Guide to the Milwaukee Road in Montana.*

22   **Early arrivers named the town:** Carter, a son of Irish immigrants and an Ohio native, came to Montana in 1882 when it was still a territory. He settled in Helena, which became the state capital seven years later when Montana achieved statehood, and began practicing law. He was elected to the U.S. Senate as a Republican and served in the chamber from 1895 until 1901. Carter gave his name to two other Montana places, the town of Carter in Choteau County and Carter County in the state's far southeast corner.

23   **Some family members:** Interview with members of Jim Muri's Family (2013).

24   **The Johnsons had two daughters:** Rosebud County Bicentennial Committee, "They Came and Stayed" (1986).

24   **Muri spread, which eventually:** Telephone interview with Kathy Muri Boutelle (2018).

24   **Friends and family remembered:** Rosebud County Bicentennial Committee.

25   **If the Muri family got:** Rosebud County Bicentennial Committee.

26   **He reportedly was scheduled:** A search of Miles City Star microfilm for the first six months of 1932 turned up no further mention of the proposed Dempsey appearance in Miles City. Also, a search of newspapers.com, an archive of digitized newspapers, turned up no mention of Dempsey as a referee in Great Falls.

27   **"We'd run the cattle":** Jim's family interview.

28   **The one-room schoolhouse:** Rosebud County Bicentennial Committee.

29   **When Jim and his brothers:** Rosebud County Bicentennial Committee.

29   **"We never had real battles":** Jim's family interview.

30   **Another memorable adventure:** Jim's family interview.

30   **The Muri brothers' escapades:** Interview with Marie Ansoms, Laurel, Montana (July 2018).

30   **A famed outfit:** *Western Horseman*, "Miles City Traditions," (August 28, 2007).

33   **His role model:** Frank W. Wiley, "Montana and the Sky; the Beginning of Aviation in the Land of the Shining Mountains" (1966).

33   **The bomber, which had:** Wiley.

33   **By 1930, airlines followed:** Bluegrass Airlines, "Feature of the Month - Centennial of Flight," (2003).

34   **As he continued his upward glance:** Robert B. Copes, "The Last Midway Marauder," (2007).

35   **Jim and his brothers traveled:** Copes.

35   **The senior Muri:** Copes.

35   **Rasmus also taught Jim:** Copes.

35   **His father encouraged that impulse:** Copes.

36   **"Many of the smaller":** Rosebud County Bicentennial Committee.

37   **In the 1930s, before:** Wikimedia Foundation, "Sugar Beet." (2018).

37   **The Muri boys' job:** Jim's family interview.

37   **He could surpass any:** Jim's family interview.

38   **"You got so stiff":** Jim's family interview.

39   **One day, he was:** Copes.

39   **One evening, for example:** Jim's family interview.

39   **Another time, basketball became:** Jim's family interview.

40   **Custer County High School:** Custer County High School, "Branding Iron," (1936 and 1930).

41   **Jim was among twenty-six boys:** "Branding Iron" (1936).

trainers produced between the 1930s and 1950s by Link Aviation Devices, of Binghamton, New York. They were used to train pilots by almost every combatant nation in World War II. Wikimedia Foundation, "Link Trainer."

67 **"So, when December 7th**: "Revenge of the Red Raiders."

68 **Japan attacked Pearl Harbor**: Wikimedia Foundation, "Attack on Pearl Harbor."

CHAPTER 6

69 **Muri's flight log**: Muri flight logs.

69 **Decades later, Jim recalled**: Marauder Society interview.

70 **Maj. Dwight D. Divine**: "Revenge of the Red Raiders."

72 **Rations finally reached the 22nd**: "Revenge of the Red Raiders."

72 **Jim reached Muroc**: Muri flight logs.

73 **One incident symbolized how**: "Revenge of the Raiders."

75 **With the 22nd somewhat**: Muri flight logs.

CHAPTER 7

77 **As 1942 began, Admiral**: Nimitz *Greybook*, p. 130

77 **Before the friends got**: Merrill Thomas Dewan, "Red Raider Diary" (e-book, 2009).

78 **At San Francisco, about 400 men**: "Revenge of the Red Raiders."

79 **Ships carrying the 22nd**: "Revenge of the Red Raiders."

79 **"All of us were dumbstruck"**: Dewan.

79 **Hulks of planes hit**: Public domain photos taken after December 7, 1941, attack showing damaged barracks,

gun emplacements, U.S. flag waving on mast; Wikimedia Foundation, "Hickam Air Force Base."

81   **On February 16, Muri:** Dewan.

82   **When Jim wrote Alice:** letters from Jim to Alice, 1942.

CHAPTER 8

88   **Bell grew up in coal-mining:** Lonnie Bell, "Slidin' Along With Lonnie Bell" (2012)

89   **Bell and his comrades:** Bell.

91   **Historian Samuel Eliot Morison:** Samuel Eliot Morison, "Coral Sea, Midway and Submarine Actions," (1950), pp. 74-75.

94   **Earlier in May, Lonnie:** Interview with Lonnie Bell (July 2017).

96   **"Thus, neither big (Japanese):** Samuel Eliot Morison, "History of United States Naval Operations in World War II" (1950), p. 174.

96   **Recalling the appearance and:** Undated document provided by Sylvia Saadati.

The narrative for Chapters 9, 10 and 11 draws on several well-known books about the Pacific Theater of World War II and the Battle of Midway that have appeared in the past 50 years, which describe the actions of Jim Muri and his *Susie-Q* crew, the other B-26s that were part of the June 4 attack, and the Navy Avengers. Martin Caidin wrote one of the first books designed for general readers; his 1966 book, *The Ragged, Rugged Warriors*, focuses on Allied air war in the Pacific and China during the early years of combat. It includes a chapter, "The Other Midway," that spotlights the sacrificial efforts of the B-26s.

Other books that mention the first wave of Army and Navy torpedo planes to hit the Japanese fleet include (original publication dates listed): Walter Lord's "Incredible Victory: The Battle of Midway" (1976); Gordon Prange's "Miracle at Midway" (1982); and, the most comprehensive of all, "A Glorious Page in Our History: The Battle of Midway 4-6 June 1942" (1992), a team effort led by Robert J. Cressman, assisted by Steve Ewing, Barrett Tillman, Mark Horgan, Clark Reynolds and Stan Cohen. Source information for details beyond that found in the overview books is listed for individual chapters.

CHAPTER 9

104   **"I got in just as:** Marauder Society interview.

105   **"What kind of a target?":** National World War II Museum, YouTube Video about Midway land attackers (2012).

107   **"Meatballs" ahead, the Americans:** U.S. servicemen called what is now an intercom an "interphone" during World War II.

CHAPTER 10

111   **"It sounded like hail":** Tom Dewan conversations.

111   **"If my momma could":** Tom Dewan; NBC Radio, "Army Hour" broadcast (June 14, 1942). On the Army Hour broadcast, Colin Villenes, co-pilot of Jim Collins' B-26, said his voice was that heard over the radio.

112   **Collins and Muri spotted *Akagi:*** University of Akron interview with Jim Muri, Jim Collins, Thomas Weams (1995).

112   **"I got the nose down":** National World War II Museum.

113 **Moore and the others:** Dewan.

CHAPTER 11

122 **Muri and Collins:** "World War II Diaries – Combat Narratives – the Battle of Midway, Battle of Midway – Supplementary Report."

124 **That recognition triggered jockeying:** James D. Hornfischer, "The Fleet At Flood Tide: American At Total War in the Pacific, 1944-1945" (2016).

CHAPTER 12

143 **Given wartime censorship:** Dewan.

144 **A few days later:** Dewan.

CHAPTER 13

153 **So, the young couple:** Dad's military chronology; phone interview with Sylvia Saadati (January 2019).

154 **"I had orders":** Marauder Society interview.

155 **The military built:** Nick Wynne, Richard Moorhead, "Florida in World War II - Floating Fortress (e-book, 2010)

156 **Their daughter, Sylvia:** phone interview with Sylvia Saadati.

158 **The federal government started:** H.H. Arnold, "Global Mission" (1949)., pp. 300-301.

161 **her brother, James:** phone interview with James R. Muri (Nov. 6, 2017).

161 **"They had this thing":** phone interview with Sylvia Saadati

163 **Muri's flight log for July 1942:** Muri flight logs.

CHAPTER 14

CHAPTER 15

CHAPTER 16

191   **In an interview conducted:** Colin D. Heaton, "Jimmy
Doolittle and the Emergence of American Air Power"
(2003).

191   **Jimmy Doolittle III, a retired:** email to author from
Jimmy Doolittle III (2018)

CHAPTER 17

193   **B-26s played a pivotal role:** Daniel Ford, "Mission to
Utah Beach," Smithsonian Air & Space Collector's
Edition (2018).

193   **Watertown, a municipal airport:** Watertown, S.D., web
site, "Watertown, S.D. History"; 445th Bomb Group web
site, "702nd Bomb Squadron Training Base."

200   **On June 5, 1947:** Dad's military chronology.

200   **The telegram said:** 2019 phone interview of Sylvia
Saadati.

203   **Production of:** Wolf, p. 141.

203   **As few as two people:** Wikimedia Foundation, "Douglas
A-26 Invader"

204   **"The house (in Great Falls)":** Sylvia Saadati phone
interview.

204   **On January 10, 1948:** Saadati.

205   **When all four Muris:** Saadati.

CHAPTER 18

211   **Jim got about a month's leave:** Dad's military
chronology.

213   **Jim's daughter, Sylvia:** 2019 interview with Sylvia
Saadati.

217   **A Dallas base:** Dad's military chronology.

217 **The Dallas NAS:** Wikimedia Foundation, "Grand Prairie Armed Forces Reserve Complex."

219 **The first to shine:** Caidin, "The Ragged, Rugged Warriors," p. 334.

219 **In the spring of:** Letter from Walter Lord to Jim Muri (May 13, 1966)

CHAPTER 19

221 **Jim might have surprised:** Saadati, 2019

CHAPTER 20

230 **Bell's accomplishments:** Bell, p. 264. Bell also was named to the Montana Broadcasters Hall of Fame in 2005 and to the Montana Cowboy Hall of Fame/Western Heritage Center in 2014.

230 **Bell spent 20 years:** Bell, "Slidin' Along with Lonnie Bell," p. 70.

233 **A few years earlier:** Bell, 106-117.

236 **Nelson, a former crop duster:** Interviews with Roger Nelson (2013, 2017).

236 **"Muri says":** Lonnie Bell interview (2017).

237 **"He started telling":** Interviews with Roger Nelson.

CHAPTER 21

240 **As Roger recalled:** Interviews with Roger Nelson.

242 **Instead, a member of the:** Copes, "The Last Midway Marauder."

242 **Leigh Wade:** A pioneering aviator who became a U.S. Air Force General and was known especially for his role in 1924, as an Army Lieutenant, as one of eight "Magellans of the Air" who made the first flight around the world.

CHAPTER 22

246   **Early recognition of:** Morison, "Coral Sea, Midway and
Submarine Actions," p. 121.

CHAPTER 23

253   **Those honored range:** Internment.net, "Eastern
Montana State Veterans Cemetery, Miles City, Montana-
Burial Records."

Bibliography

Note: Newspaper articles used as sources are cited in the text but not listed here, with the exception of a special-edition article about Midway published in the *New York Times*.

BOOKS

Arnold, H.H., General of the Air Force. *Global Mission*. New York: Harper & Brothers, 1949.

Bell, Lonnie and Harold Hollingsworth. *Slidin' Along With Lonnie Bell*. Billings, MT: KGHL Radio AM-790, 2012.

Bicheno, Hugh. *Midway*. London: Cassell & Co, 2001.

Caidin, Martin. *The Ragged, Rugged Warriors*. New York: Bantam Books, 1985.

Committee, Rosebud County Bicentennial. *They Came and Stayed*. Rosebud County Bicentennial Committee, 1986.

Cressman, Robert J., Steve Ewing, Barrett Tillman, Mark Horan, Clark Reynolds, and Stan Cohen. *A Glorious Page in Our History: The Battle of Midway 4-6 June 1942*. Missoula, MT: Pictorial Histories Publishing Company, 1992.

Dewan, Merrill Thomas. *Red Raider Diary*. Pittsburg, Pennsylvania: Rose Dog Books, 2009.

Doolittle, James Harold and Caroll V. Glines. *I Could Never be So Lucky Again: An Autobiography*. New York: Bantam Books, 1991.

Evans, Don, Walter Gaylord, Harry A. Nelson, Lawrence J. Hickey. *Eagles Over the Pacific: Revenge of the Red Raiders*. Boulder, Colorado: International Research and Publishing Corporation, 2006. Kindle.

Hornfischer, James D. *The Fleet At Flood Tide: American At Total War in the Pacific, 1944-1945*. Bantam, 2016.

Johnson, E.R. *Widow Maker: A Novel of World War II*. Lumina Press, 2017. Kindle.

Lord, Walter. *Incredible Victory: The Battle of Midway*. Short Hills, NJ: Buford Books, 1998.

Lundstrom, John B. *The First Team Pacific: Naval Air Combat From Pearl Harbor to Midway*. Annapolis, MD: Naval Institute Press, 1984.

Marston, Daniel. *The Pacific War: From Pearl Harbor to Hiroshima*. Oxford: Osprey, 2005.

McCarter, Steve. *Guide to the Milwaukee Road in Montana*. Helena: Montana Historical Society Press, 1992.

Morison, Samuel Eliot. *The Two-Ocean War, a Short History of the United States Navy in the Second World War*. Boston: Boston, Little, Brown, 1963.

Morison, Samuel Eliot. *History of United States Naval Operations in World War II, Volume IV, Coral Sea, Midway and Submarine Actions, May 1942-August 1942*. Boston: Little, Brown, 1950.

Parshall, Jonathan B. and Anthony P. Tully. *Shattered Sword: The Untold Story of the Battle of Midway*. Washington: Potomac Books, 2007.

Prange, Gordon William. *Miracle At Midway*. McGraw-Hill, 1982. Kindle.

Symonds, Craig L. *The Battle of Midway*. New York: Oxford University Press, 2011. Kindle.

Wiley, Frank W. *Montana and the Sky; the Beginning of Aviation in the Land of the Shining Mountains*. Helena: Helena Montana Aeronautics Commission, 1966.

Wolf, William. *Martin B-26 Marauder: The Ultimate Look, From Drawing Board to Widow Maker Vindicated*. Atglen, PA: Schiffer Publishing, 2014.

Wynne, Nick; Moorhead, Richard. *Florida in World War II - Floating Fortress*. Charleston, S.C.: The History Press, 2010. Kindle.

INTERVIEWS

Ransoms, Marie, personal conversation with the author, Laurel, Montana, July 29, 2018.

Bell, Lonnie, personal conversation with the author, Billings, Montana, July 2017.

Boutelle, Kathy Muri, telephone conversation with the author, 2018.

Dewan, Thomas, phone conversations with the author, May 21, May 22, 2019.

Doolittle, Jimmy, "Jimmy Doolittle and the Emergence of American Airpower," interview by Colin D. Heaton, September 27, 1993, published May 2003, Academic Search Elite database.

Family of Jim Muri, discussion with the author, Miles City, Montana, May 27, 2013.

Magruder, Marshall, personal conversation with the author, Billings, Montana, July 2017

Muri, James P., interview by Dick Ellinger, representative of B-26 Marauder Historical Society, Reedpoint, Montana, August 10, 1990.

Muri, James R., telephone conversation with the author, November 6, 2017.

Nelson, Roger, personal conversations with the author, 2013, 2017.

Saadati, Sylvia, telephone and personal conversations with the author, 2013 through 2019.

University of Akron, interviews with Jim Muri, Jim Collins, Thomas Weams, 1995.

WEBSITES

"22nd Bomb Group - the Red Raiders in Australia During Ww2." http://www.ozatwar.com/22ndbomb.htm.

"Chanute Air Force Base."

>https://en.m.wikipedia.org/wiki/Chanute_Air_Force_Base.

"Chapter 18 - the Great Depression Transforms Montana, 1929-1941."
Montana: Stories of the Land 2018.
http://svcalt.mt.gov/education/textbook/Chapter18/Chapter18
.asp.

"Command Summary of Fleet Admiral Chester W. Nimitz, USN -
Nimitz "Greybook"." *Covering the Period 7 December 1941 to 31
August 1942* 1 of 8 (1942): Accessed March 19, 2019,
http://www.ibiblio.org/anrs/graybook.html.

"Eastern Montana State Veterans Cemetery, Miles City, Montana - Burial
Records."
http://www.interment.net/data/us/mt/custer/veteran_east/ind
ex.htm.

"Feature of the Month - Centennial of Flight." Bluegrass Airlines (2003).
Bluegrassairlines.com

"Hickam Air Force Base."
https://en.m.wikipedia.org/wiki/Hickam_Air_Force_Base

National World War II Museum. YouTube video about Midway land
attackers (2012): https://youtu.be/jIHUKirztSY.

Pacific Wrecks. "A-24 Dive Bomber Serial Number 41-15798."
https://www.pacificwrecks.com/aircraft/a-24/41-15798.html.

"Sugar Beet." (2018): 2018. https://en.wikipedia.org/wiki/Sugar_beet.

"Synopsis of the Battle of Midway (3-7 June 1942)." Naval History Blog
(2013): https://www.navalhistory.org/2013/06/03/synopsis-of-
the-battle-of-midway-3-7-june-1942

"George Calnan." Accessed 2018,
https://en.wikipedia.org/wiki/George_Calnan.

lympic Museum, "The Olympic Oath: 1920-1980." http://olympic-
museum.de/oath/theoath.htm.

'oday in Texas History."
https://blog.chron.com/tXpotomac/2010/06/today-in-Texas-
history-Randolph-air-force-base-dedication. June 20, 2010.

ikimedia Foundation. "423d Bombardment Squadron."
https://en.m.wikipedia.org/wiki/423d_Bombardment_Squadron

ikimedia Foundation. "Attack on Pearl Harbor."
https://en.wikipedia.org/wiki/Attack_on_Pearl_Harbor

ikimedia Foundation. "Big Week/operation Argument."
https://en.wikipedia.org/wiki/Big_Week.

ikimedia Foundation. "Douglas A-26 Invader." Accessed March 22,
2019, https://en.wikipedia.org/wiki/Douglas_A-26_Invader

ikimedia Foundation. "Grand Prairie Armed Forces Reserve
Complex." 2019.
https://en.wikipedia.org/wiki/Grand_Prairie_Armed_Forces_R
eserve_Complex

'ikimedia Foundation, Wikimedia. "Link Trainer,"
https://en.m.wikipedia.org/wiki/Link_Trainer

'ikimedia Foundation. "Louisiana Maneuvers"
https://en.wikipedia.org/wiki/Louisiana_Maneuvers.

'ikimedia Foundation. "Stalag Luft 1."
https://en.wikipedia.org/wiki/Stalag_Luft_I

Xc124314 · Laysan Albatross · Phoebastria Immutabilis."
https://www.naturesoundmap.com/listing/laysan-albatross/

ERIODICALS

bbott, Jonathan. "The Last Ride of Susie-Q." *Ghost Wings* (2006).

ir Age Inc. "Martin B-26 Marauder." (1945).

Morison, Samuel Eliot, "Two Minutes That Changed the Pacific War." *New York Times*, 1952.

Guttman, Jon. "Marauder At Midway." *Aviation History* (2005).

Popular Mechanics. "The Army Asked for a Miracle. The Answer Was the B-26." (1943).

Pratt, Fletcher. "The Mysteries of Midway." *Harpers* (two-part series that appeared in July, August 1943).

Western Horseman. "Miles City Traditions." (August 28, 2007).

OTHER SOURCES

"Army Radio Hour Broadcast." (1942): NBC Radio, archived in the Library of Congress, obtained by Ray Carver, nephew of B-26 crewman Ernest Mohon and provided to author with NBC permission.

"B-26 "Suzy-Q" Serial Number 40-1391."

Custer County High School, Miles City, Montana. *Branding Iron.* (School yearbook) 1930, 1936.

Copes, Robert B. "The Last Midway Marauder." "Research Report Submitted to the Faculty in Partial Fulfillment of the Graduation Requirements." Maxwell Air Force Base, Alabama (April 2007).

"Dad's Chronology Document - email message from Sylvia Saadati to author." February 2017.

Magruder, Marshall. "June 4 1942 Timeline." B-26 Marauder Historical Society 2018 Gathering (2018).

Muri, James P. "Letters From Jim Muri to Alice Muri." (1941, 1942).

Muri, Jim. "Postcard." (1936). Card provided by Sylvia Saadati.

"Old Buddies." Card provided by Sylvia Saadati.

Custer County High School. "High School Aviation Studies." (1935):

National Public Radio, "World War II Pilot Was Initially Embarrassed By Hero Status After Battle of Midway." (2013).

wartz, Henry. Letters (1940, 1941)

World War II Diaries - Combat Narratives - the Battle of Midway,
     Battle of Midway - Supplementary Report."
     https://www.history.navy.mil/research/library/online-reading-
     room/title-list-alphabetically/b/battle-of-midway-3-6-june-1942-
     combat-narrative.html

Index

Barksdale Air Field, 69
Barnacle, Gerald B., 144, 150
Battle of the Coral Sea, 87, 92, 95, 233, 263, 269, 272
Beartooth Mountains, 222, 229, 234, 236
Bell, Lonnie, 13, 87, 94, 136, 229, 232, 238, 240, 263, 268, 271
Best, Dick, 245
Big Timber, Montana, 58, 141, 221, 222, 226, 234, 235, 239
Biggs Field, 69
Billings, 9, 10, 26, 29, 33, 38, 41, 50, 87, 88, 136, 169, 173, 175, 221, 224, 225, 229, 230, 231, 234, 235, 236, 237, 239, 240, 242, 251, 252, 253, 271, 273
Blue Army, 63
Boutelle, Kathy Muri, 258
Bragg, Addison, 223, 225
Brett, George H., 51
Bridger Creek, 135, 221, 222, 226, 233, 234, 235, 236, 239
Brown, Taylor, 237
Brussels, 213
Bunch, Clare, 182, 189
Burnett, Vince, 184
Bush, George H.W., 243
Cabbage Patch, 211
Calderwood, Tom, 66, 261
Calnan, George, 44, 260, 274
Camel cigarettes, 105, 108

Camp Drake, 205, 209
Carolina maneuvers, 66
Carter, Thomas H., 23, 257
Carterville, 21, 22, 23, 24, 25, 26, 28, 29, 30, 31, 34, 36, 38, 42, 55, 84, 144, 153, 187, 201, 216, 226
Casablanca Conference, 179
Chanute Field, 45, 55, 128, 136
Chanute, Octave, 55
Choctawhatchee Bay, 158
Collins, Jim, 18, 103, 117, 121, 148, 224, 264, 273
Colt .45 pistol, 207
Combined Fleet, 91, 102, 103
Cooper, Don, 231, 237
Cooper, John E., 73
Copes, Robert B., 242, 259, 268, 276
Cotton Bowl, 217
Crazy Mountains, 222
Curtis, Tony, 34, 241, 242
Dallas Naval Air Station, 217, 218
Darque, H.A., 63, 64
Dayton, 129, 144, 154, 189
D-Day, 168, 193, 247
Dempsey, Jack, 25, 26, 258
Denton, Jeremiah, 243
Dewan, 13, 75, 77, 78, 79, 81, 82, 131, 143, 144, 218, 262, 263, 264, 265, 271, 273

www.ingramcontent.com/pod-product-compliance
Lightning Source LLC
Chambersburg PA
CBHW051846090426

42811CB00034B/2234/J